PAYING FOR CITIES

The Search for Sustainable Municipal Revenues

INSTITUTE FOR PUBLIC ECONOMICS

Paying for Cities

The Search for Sustainable Municipal Revenues

Western Studies in Economic Policy No. 9

EDITED BY PAUL BOOTHE

Published by
The Institute for Public Economics
Department of Economics
8–14 HM Tory Building
University of Alberta
Edmonton, Alberta
T6G 2H4

Copyright © 2003 The Institute for Public Economics
Printed in Canada
ISBN 1–55195–182–7

NATIONAL LIBRARY OF CANADA CATALOGUING IN PUBLICATION

    Paying for cities : the search for sustainable municipal revenues / edited by Paul Boothe.

(Western studies in economic policy ; no. 9)
Papers presented at a conference held at the University of Alberta, Nov. 2002.
Includes bibliographical references.
ISBN 1-55195-182-7

    1. Municipal revenue—Alberta—Congresses. 2. Municipal finance—Alberta—Congresses. 3. Fiscal policy—Alberta—Congresses. 4. Municipal finance—Canada—Congresses. I. Boothe, Paul Michael, 1954-   II. University of Alberta. Institute for Public Economics. III. Series.

HJ9351.P39 2003   336.02'7123   C2003-905615-5

All rights reserved.
No part of this publication may be produced, stored in a retrieval system, or transmitted in any form or by any means, electronic, mechanical, photocopying, recording, or otherwise, without the prior permission of the copyright owner.

∞ Printed on acid-free paper.

 Institute for Public Economics

Contents

VII **ACKNOWLEDGEMENTS**

IX **INTRODUCTION**
PAUL BOOTHE

1 **CONTROLLING THE CREATURES**
An Historical Perspective on Financing Cities
J.C. HERBERT EMERY

17 **COMMENTS ON "AN HISTORICAL PERSPECTIVE"**
ALLISON D. O'BRIEN

19 **FINANCING CITIES AND FISCAL SUSTAINABILITY**
HARRY M. KITCHEN

37 **COMMENTS ON "FINANCING CITIES AND FISCAL SUSTAINABILITY"**
EDWARD C. LeSAGE

43 **REMOVING THE SHACKLES**
Some Modest, and Some Immodest, Proposals to Pay for Cities
RONALD D. KNEEBONE AND KENNETH J. McKENZIE

79 **COMMENTS ON "REMOVING THE SHACKLES"**
BEV DAHLBY

83 **THE POLITICS OF PAYING FOR CITIES IN CANADA**
ROBERT YOUNG

99 **COMMENTS ON "THE POLITICS OF PAYING FOR CITIES IN CANADA"**
GILES GHERSON

105 **RAPPORTEUR: WHAT HAVE WE LEARNED?**
MELVILLE L. McMILLAN

123 **CONTRIBUTORS**

Acknowledgements

THE INSTITUTE FOR PUBLIC ECONOMICS (IPE) is pleased to publish *Paying for Cities: The Search for Sustainable Municipal Revenues*. This volume, which focuses on critical financing issues facing municipal governments, represents a new and important dimension of IPE's mandate to promote public discussion of fiscal policy issues in Alberta and beyond. The essays contained in this volume were first presented at a conference held in November 2002 at the University of Alberta. I would like to thank the government of Alberta for its financial support, the Honourable Guy Boutilier, Minister of Municipal Affairs, for opening the conference, and Brad Pickering, Deputy Minister of Municipal Affairs, and Peter Kruselnicki, Deputy Minister of Finance, for their help with planning the event. I am also grateful to Dawn Bissett and Trish Filevich for their work on logistics and publicity for the conference. Finally, thanks to our excellent copyeditor, Carol Berger, for contributing the essential editing and publication help needed to bring the project to completion.

Introduction

THE IMPORTANCE OF CITIES to the economic and social development of nations has become an article of faith among both scholars and policymakers. In Canada, some of the pioneering work on this issue has been done by Thomas Courchene and Colin Telmer of Queen's University in their book *From Heartland to North American Region State: The Social, Fiscal and Federal Evolution of Ontario*. If cities are such important generators of wealth and well-being, how we pay for them must be important too.

A number of factors have come together to bring about what municipal leaders characterize as a crisis in municipal finance. As Canadian federal and provincial governments struggled to eliminate their deficits in the mid-1990s, one of the key strategies used was to cut transfers. Cities could not escape the fallout from the reduction in financial support. Further, the ongoing migration of Canadians from rural areas and smaller communities to urban centres put additional pressure on cities to provide infrastructure and other services at a time when resources were constrained. Finally, as part of their strategy for dealing with reduced transfers, provinces and cities postponed maintenance of essential infrastructure.

Municipal leaders have put a great deal of effort into making provincial and federal governments as well as the public aware of this issue. They argue that current tax bases are insufficient to meet the revenue needs of cities and that access to additional resources are needed. Further, these additional resources must be stable and predictable. Typically, this means either additional grants from provinces or the federal government and/or revenue sharing of existing taxes (for example, gasoline-tax revenue). Of course, other things being equal, governments would always prefer that someone else raised the revenue that they spend, but that does not mean that municipal arguments are without merit.

The purpose of this volume is to contribute to the debate on municipal finance in Canada by reporting on the proceedings of a conference organized by the University of Alberta's Institute for Public Economics in November 2002. The conference was generously supported by grants from Alberta Finance and Alberta Municipal Affairs and attracted leading researchers from across Canada, as well as officials from all three levels of government. The conference led to a wide-ranging discussion of how we should pay for cities. It is our hope that the analysis summarized in this volume will make a useful contribution to finding practical solutions to this important public policy issue.

SUMMARY

The volume begins with University of Calgary Professor J.C. Herbert Emery's historical perspective on Canadian cities. Emery notes the change in the relative fiscal importance of municipalities in the Canadian federation over the past 75 years, with provinces and the federal government growing substantially in fiscal importance relative to cities. He argues that this change has occurred as a result of an expansion of the social programs offered by provinces and the federal government, rather than a transfer of responsibilities from municipal governments.

Emery also focuses on the constitutional status of municipalities as "creatures" of the provinces—much like school and hospital boards. Compared to these other "creatures of the provinces," municipalities enjoy a relatively large degree of autonomy. However, in many cases this autonomy does not extend to complete freedom in raising revenue or borrowing.

In concluding his essay, Emery leaves us with three questions to consider in examinations of municipal finance: 1) Should cities have more responsibilities and autonomy in raising revenues? 2) Should cities rely more heavily on debt financing? and 3) Should the tax mix available to cities be altered to included provincial sales taxes?

Allison D. O'Brien, from the University of Alberta's Institute for Public Economics, begins his commentary on the Emery essay by addressing the three questions posed in Emery's conclusion. O'Brien argues that there may be an argument for expanding the responsibilities of municipalities—especially in the area of social programs like health care, education and social assistance—in those cases where provincial efforts to "regionalize" services have met with mixed success.

On the question of whether or not municipalities should be permitted more access to borrowing, O'Brien calls for more research, and suggests that it may be fruitful to compare Alberta's experience with that of British Columbia, where the provincial municipal finance authority borrows on the "full credit of the provincial municipal tax base."

Finally, on the question of whether or not the mix of municipal revenues should be altered, O'Brien argues in favour of the status quo based on his belief that the property tax is the most appropriate revenue stream to fund most municipal services. In concluding his commentary, O'Brien draws attention to the desirable equalization of school funding that is accomplished through the education property tax, and recommends that a system of municipal tax equalization be investigated.

The second study of the conference was presented by Professor Harry M. Kitchen of Trent University. Kitchen begins by highlighting the importance of cities as generators of economic activity and wealth in Canada. Governments make an important contribution to the ability of cities to fulfil this role. This is because the mix of taxes and services governments choose are important determinants of where firms and skilled workers decide to locate.

Kitchen argues that current financing arrangements are not sufficient to sustain cities as wealth generators and that an extended range of strategies will be needed. He puts forward three options that could be considered to provide sustainable funding for cities:

- Revenue bonds—municipal governments borrow for revenue-generating infrastructure projects (i.e., toll roads, bridges and public transportation) and pay interest and principal from the proceeds of operating the infrastructure.
- Tax-exempt bonds—provinces and the federal government exempt municipal bonds from tax and therefore reduce the cost of municipal borrowing. This scheme likely involves a transfer from all taxpayers to city property taxpayers.
- Tax incremental financing districts—municipalities dedicate the proceeds of incremental property tax to redevelopment in neighbourhoods that require revitalization.

In his commentary on the Kitchen article, Professor Edward C. LeSage of the University of Alberta suggests that the crisis of city financing may be the result not of faulty intergovernmental fiscal relations but of structurally derived weak municipal leadership. In his view, provinces may have an interest in municipal governments remaining politically weak as these governments are potential rivals for the allegiance of provincial voters. This interest is promoted through nonpartisan councils, a divisive ward system and other representation schemes. LeSage opines that one barrier to progress on sustainable municipal financing is "our deficit of civic leadership."

The third study of the volume, by Professor Ronald D. Kneebone and Professor Kenneth J. McKenzie of the University of Calgary, focuses on how municipalities have adapted to the federal and provincial deficit offloading that occurred in 1990s. Kneebone and McKenzie note that provincial cuts to municipal transfers have been concentrated on unconditional transfers; provinces have reduced both the resources and flexibility available to municipalities.

They consider proposals to increase municipal revenues and group them under two headings: modest (proposals that can be implemented within current structures) and immodest (proposals that would require substantive changes to existing fiscal arrangements). Modest proposals are based on the benefit principle of taxation—the principle that governments should try to collect the required revenue from those who reap the benefits of public services. Under this heading, Kneebone and McKenzie include expanded use of user fees, property taxes and, to fund transportation infrastructure, allowing municipalities to levy excise taxes on fuel.

Under the heading of immodest proposals, Kneebone and McKenzie propose that municipalities be given access to a provincial sales tax or a business value-added (BVA) tax. Kneebone and McKenzie conclude with a plea for more municipal flexibility in revenue raising in order to give local governments a level of political clout that matches their contribution as revenue generators in the Canadian federation.

In his commentary on the Kneebone and McKenzie article, Professor Bev Dahlby of the University of Alberta begins by asking if we are we looking at the right data. He notes that Kneebone and McKenzie's analysis is based on data for all local government that includes both rural municipalities as well as the largest cities. Dahlby wonders whether or not we would get a better view of the issues if we focused on data for, say, the fifteen largest Canadian cities. Indeed, some of the ideas proposed by Kneebone and McKenzie are probably appropriate for the largest cities, but are inappropriate for smaller cities, towns and rural areas.

Dahlby also expresses concern over the impact of the Kneebone and McKenzie proposals on accountability and incentives for good fiscal behaviour. This is a special concern with revenue-sharing proposals like the BVA tax. Despite the concerns expressed, however, Dahlby believes that some of the proposals advanced by Kneebone and McKenzie may be better than the status quo and thus merit further analysis.

In the volume's final essay, Professor Robert Young of the University of Western Ontario provides a political analysis of the municipal finance issue and considers the likelihood that substantial change will occur in the current political environment. He starts from the premise that cities need to wrest additional powers and resources from provincial and federal governments in order to match their recent expanded stature as wealth generators in Canada.

Young examines the policymaking environment and how it has changed, the impact of demographic change, including immigration and rural migration to urban areas, as well as the role of political actors. His analysis leads him to conclude that the current fiscal arrangements are politically "efficient" and thus no bold new initiatives are likely to be implemented.

The political efficiency that he refers to stems in part from the high degree of accountability of municipal government—the result of a close matching of the benefits and costs of government programs.

In Young's view, one way to improve the current situation for municipalities would be for federal and provincial governments to refrain from pushing additional, unfunded spending mandates on municipalities. Further, Young advocates expanded revenue sharing with municipalities and tax relief for municipal debt.

In his commentary, Giles Gherson of the *Edmonton Journal* finds he is largely in agreement with Robert Young. Gherson focuses on the expenditure side and argues that we are witnessing a significant deterioration in services in large cities. In part, he argues that the cause of the problem is fragmentation. Gherson points to the fact that there are 22 municipalities in the Edmonton region alone. He also shares Young's view that major changes are unlikely in the near term and wonders, like LeSage, what changes in political institutions might lead to stronger leadership at the municipal level.

As rapporteur for the conference, it was left to Professor Melville L. McMillan of the University of Alberta to draw common threads from the essays, as well as to highlight areas of controversy. McMillan argues that while municipal finance is not in crisis, there is substantial room for improvement. He also notes that relatively little attention was paid by the authors to the rationalization of existing grants, and he argues that there may be substantial returns to efforts in that direction.

McMillan argues against proposals for tax-exempt bonds because of the distortions they engender, and suggests that income-tax deductions for property taxes for owner-occupants might be preferable. He agrees with giving cities access to the provincial excise tax on gasoline to fund transportation expenditures, but outlines a number of problems that might occur if municipalities levied their own excise taxes. In conclusion, McMillan argues that solutions to the municipal finance problem may not require an increase in overall tax burdens. Instead, he writes, the problem could be resolved by ensuring that municipalities get access to an appropriate share of stable funding.

Paul Boothe
Professor and Director, Institute for Public Economics
University of Alberta

EnCana Scholar in Public Policy
C.D. Howe Institute

J.C. HERBERT EMERY

Controlling the Creatures

An Historical Perspective on Financing Cities

BECAUSE THEY HAVE NO CONSTITUTIONALLY DESIGNATED spending or revenue responsibilities, cities are frequently referred to as creatures of the provinces. While they are not formally a third level of government, cities are important vehicles through which the provinces deliver a wide range of publicly provided goods and services. A century ago, cities and other municipalities were largely feral creatures, as local governments were largely self-supporting and relied on their own revenues and capacity to borrow to pay for expenditures. Municipal governments in aggregate had higher revenues and higher expenditures than provincial governments, despite the fact that the majority of Canadians did not live in urban communities. Today, while the majority of Canadians live in urban areas, local government spending is less than one-quarter of total provincial expenditures. Provincial governments also exert more control over their "creatures" by regulating local government borrowing and providing transfers to local governments to finance infrastructure and support municipal spending.

The difficulty with these changes in the relative role of local government is that, as Vander Ploeg (2001) argues, population growth and the pressures of a growing economy are now more of a burden for cities than a benefit. Currently, cities pay for the growth while senior levels of government reap the rewards. Thus, the combination of the rise in the potential political influence of urban voters, the increased reliance on senior levels of government and the strong growth of urban economies is creating pressure to evaluate the appropriate relationship between local governments and their overseers, the provincial governments. Mirroring the fiscal federalism debates around the division of powers and revenues between the federal and provincial governments, local governments are calling for changes in their relationship with the provincial governments. These changes are considered necessary if cities are to have the revenues needed to finance infrastructure needs and to pay for services while at the same time maintaining their political autonomy.

In this article, I examine a long-run view of the role and functions of municipal governments in Canada. I discuss developments in the institutional context that frames municipal governance, in what cities do, and in how cities have financed what they do. I discuss the changes in the importance of local governments relative to provincial governments. I also highlight technological change in transportation and the urbanization of the Canadian population, both of which have driven changes in demand for public goods and services, and how they have been supplied.

THE BIG CHANGES IN LOCAL GOVERNMENT SINCE CONFEDERATION ... OR EARLIER

What local governments can do, how they can do it, what local governments exist and their boundaries are all determined by provincial governments (Bird and Tassonyi 2002). Hanson (1952, 242) observed:

> Careful consideration must accordingly be given to provincial-municipal fiscal relations. The municipalities are agents delegated to perform functions which are provincial constitutionally; the provincial government cannot afford to regard itself as separate from its creatures.

The basic framework for Canadian municipalities was put in place in Upper Canada in 1849 with the Municipal Corporations Act, or Baldwin Act, that delineated municipal authority to levy taxes, spend and approve by-laws over local matters ranging from municipal infrastructure like roads and bridges to the licensing of taverns (Sancton 1999). The British North America Act of 1867 allocated powers and responsibilities of government between the federal and provincial governments, but local governments were not explicitly recognized in the act beyond being creations and responsibilities of the provinces. Amongst many of its provisions, Section 92 of the BNA Act assigns to the provincial legislatures the responsibilities for "the establishment, maintenance, and management of hospitals, asylums, charities," "Municipal Institutions in the Province," and "Shop, saloon, tavern, auctioneer, and other licenses in order to the raising of a Revenue for Provincial, Local, or Municipal Purposes."

The provinces conferred powers to local government explicitly through statutes, thus, municipalities are "creatures of the provinces." For example, in some cases the early responsibilities for hospitals and charities were given to municipalities while revenue-raising powers remained with the province. In some cases, municipal powers and responsibilities were assigned prior to the creation of provinces. For example, Edmonton and Calgary obtained their charters in the 1880s and had greater powers (such as the right to borrow) than the territorial government of the day. With the creation of the province of Alberta in 1905, the charters of the two major cities carried forward.

Since 1990, provincial governments in Alberta, Manitoba, Saskatchewan, Ontario and Nova Scotia have developed legislation to broaden and strengthen municipal powers by giving the cities powers within broad spheres of jurisdiction. These changes are intended to free municipalities from the burdens of provincial regulation and grant them general powers of governance: "Instead of stating what a municipality can do, the legislation assumes the legitimate range of municipal activity is very broad, so it simply says what a municipality cannot do."[1] Despite these attempts to change the status and roles of local governments in Canada, the nineteenth-century institutional structure is proving hard to change. A recent Alberta Court of Appeal decision that the City of Calgary did not have legitimate power to limit the number of taxi licences in the city rejected the broad outlines of municipal powers in the 1994 Municipal Government Act, citing an 1895 decision that "municipal corporations in the exercise of the statutory powers conferred on them to make bylaws should be confined strictly within the limits of their authority and all attempts on their part to exceed it should be fully repelled by the Courts" (Local Government Bulletin No. 30, September 2002).

Spending Responsibilities

When it comes to the spending responsibilities of local governments, there are not many surprises. The range of assigned responsibilities has varied across the provinces and over time but local governments in Canada have some involvement in expenditures like education, transportation, planning, protection to persons and property, health and social assistance, housing, industry and tourism, and recreation and culture (e.g., parks, libraries, recreation centres) (Bird and Slack, 1993). The structure of local government can be multi-tiered and spending responsibilities are apportioned across the tiers. For example, Tassonyi (1994) describes Ontario's current arrangements whereby regional, county and metropolitan Toronto are upper-tier governments, while the constituent municipalities are lower-tier municipal governments.

Regional councils in Ontario have responsibility for police, health and social services, solid waste disposal, sewer and water treatment and capital borrowing. Lower-tier municipalities normally have responsibility for fire protection, recreation, municipal hydro services, public transit (in some cases), tax collection, libraries and licensing. The levels share responsibility for services like roads, planning, sewer and water services and economic development.

In Alberta, for much of the province's history, municipal spending responsibilities were defined under the Towns and Villages Act. For example, the 1955 Act listed the following responsibilities:

- Any required maintenance of roads, highways, ditches, bridges, public parks, walks, cemeteries, parking spaces, ferries, dams, pipes or anything with respect to the water supply;
- Local airport;
- Temporary roads required for construction and any compensation to the landowners where the roads must be built;
- Local judge's salary;
- Any sign or device required for the regulation of traffic (stop lights, no-parking signs, speed limits, etc.);
- Anything required for fire protection, such as purchasing equipment, property, building of firehouse and firewalls;
- Regulating cats and dogs with the appointment of a poundkeeper whose salary is paid by the local government;
- Police enforcement, salaries, buildings and equipment;
- Annual grants to local hospitals;
- Annual grants to local doctors;
- Garbage disposal and collection;
- Water works and sewage;
- Any cost associated with testing the local milk for disease and quality (specifically to do with contagious abortion disease);
- Maintenance of gas or water piping;
- Grants to the Canadian Red Cross, Veterans' Organization, Agricultural Societies, Boards of Trade, and Incorporated Mechanics' and Literary Institutes;
- To aid needy residents of the local area;
- Public utilities such as electric lights, heat, power, natural gas and gas plants.

Over the last century there have been only a few substantive changes in municipal spending responsibilities and some have been implemented via changes in interpretation of the responsibility, as opposed to explicit or wholesale change in the level of government responsible for the spending. For example, while the provincial and federal governments have taken over the spending responsibilities for unemployment relief (via employment insurance), pensions and health care, municipalities did not abdicate the responsibility to "aid needy residents of the local area," as evidenced by Vander Ploeg's (2002) recommendation that the responsibility for any programs with a redistributive element be taken over by the provincial or federal governments. In essence, it was not the municipal responsibility for the local needy that changed, but the definition of who the local needy are (Struthers 1983, 1994).

Before 1940, aiding needy residents of the "local area" left responsibility for helping those individuals without employment, the old and the infirm, and the disabled with municipal governments. Local governments provided direct relief to such individuals after imposing means tests on income, assets and family resources for supporting the individual. Vagrants, other transients and "non-British Subjects" were clearly defined as not being local residents (or at least as not eligible for relief). In the case of vagrants, the police and court systems were used to help them on their way out of the community. The benefit of this assignment of responsibility was that, prior to 1930, the size of the population in need was not large and, consequently, neither was the expenditure. Further, local administration was a vital part of means testing as local agents could assess and monitor claims.

With the onset of the Great Depression, a large and mobile needy population moved from community to community looking for work and, increasingly, relief payments. Further, with the collapse of the prices for agricultural commodities and bank foreclosures on farms, rural residents migrated to the urban centres and often needed relief payments. The mobility of the needy population in the 1930s and the revealed weakness of the property tax base for meeting these expenditures, as many property owners went into arrears on their taxes, resulted in the movement of this primary relief responsibility away from the municipalities and up to the provincial and federal governments through the creation of unemployment insurance and old-age pensions. For example, in 1950, the province of Alberta relieved municipalities of their shares of basic old-age pensions and the municipal shares of hospitalization and medical care of old-age pensioners.

The province also took on a larger share of spending on mother's allowances and contributed 60 per cent of costs of child welfare services and indigent relief, all of which were designated municipal responsibilities.[2] While responsibility for health and social assistance has been, to a large extent, taken over by the provincial and federal governments, the responsibility for needy local residents still remains for many municipalities but it involves a much more narrowly defined population and services like social services, homeless shelters and social housing (Bird and Slack 1993).

The other important changes are in the responsibilities for grants to local doctors and hospitals. With the development of public health insurance in Canada, the provinces have also taken over the lion's share of responsibility for paying physicians and providing capital, like hospitals, for the health-care sector. Where municipalities continue to operate hospitals or ambulance services, they seldom have the responsibility to pay for them (Bird and Slack 1993).

Spending on roads and highways has always involved some amount of cost sharing between provincial and local governments. For example, Boothe and Edwards (2002) note that in 1918 legislation in Alberta classified provincial highways as "main, district and local." The province was to pay 75 per cent of the construction costs of main highways, 25 per cent of district highways and the cost of local highways were to be borne by local authorities. In 1951, the province increased its share of construction costs of secondary highways from 60 per cent to 75 per cent, and the province agreed to maintain all such roads. There were also special agreements made between municipal governments and the province for the province to contribute to the maintenance of highways running through urban centres. As part of cost-cutting measures in the 1990s, the Klein and Harris governments offloaded responsibility for many secondary highways to local governments. Alberta has recently seen the provincial government reassume responsibility for these costs.

Responsibility for local roads has turned out to be a major cost associated with population and economic growth for cities. In 1951, total expenditures on roads and highways by the provincial governments (including subsidies and grants in aid to municipalities) were $288 million, while the total of municipal expenditures was $23 million. By 1976 provincial government spending on roads and highways was $2.6 billion while spending by municipalities was $1.5 billion. Over a 25-year period, the ratio of provincial to municipal road and highway spending fell from 12.5 to 1.7. In all likelihood, this gap has closed further as the growth of road mileage under municipal jurisdiction has dramatically outpaced the growth of road mileage under provincial jurisdiction since 1976. Consider that the ratio of the total length of provincial roads to the total length of municipal roads has fallen from 0.5 in 1976 to 0.35 in 1997.[3]

Revenues and Borrowing

Before World War II, the principal revenue sources for municipalities to finance current and capital expenditures were real property taxes, business taxes, transfers from provincial governments and debt.[4] Tassonyi (1994) calculates that between 1913 and 1937 almost 80 per cent of total revenues of Ontario municipalities came from property taxes. By 1991, the revenue base of municipalities in Canada had considerably diversified: 31 per cent of municipal revenues in Canada were from property taxes, 37 per cent were from transfers to municipalities and the remaining 31 per cent came from other sources of revenue, such as sales of goods and services, rentals, concessions and franchises, licenses and permits, remittances from own enterprises, interest, interest and penalties on taxes, fines, other miscellaneous revenues (Bird and Slack 1993). For many municipal services, user fees, in particular, have become important sources of revenue (Vander Ploeg 2002).

The rising importance of transfer payments from provincial governments to local governments has created the problem of local government dependence on the decisions of the senior level of government. As most provincial-municipal grants in Canada are conditional (for a specific purpose or project), the provincial authorities can exert considerable control over local expenditures. The provinces can impose rules and regulations over how the money is spent and, in some cases, alter the prices of some services provided to the municipality (Bird and Slack 1993). The use of conditional grants, and supervision of municipal spending by provincial governments, was the outcome of experiences during fiscal crises, such as the 1930s, that highlighted the reality that, as "creatures of the provinces," the provinces were responsible for the consequences of local government spending decisions (Bird and Tassonyi 2001).

Prior to 1930, local governments financed infrastructure needs with debt and current revenues. The character of much of this investment was that it was being built "ahead of demand." Expectations for future needs for infrastructure, or profitability of investments, were high over the wheat boom period from 1896 to 1911 as Canada's economy surged with the emergence of the western wheat economy and rapid population growth. Consequently, levels of provincial and municipal indebtedness rose, and the federal government promoted the construction of two ultimately doomed transcontinental railways with loan guarantees for the railway bonds. Boothe and Edwards (2002) describe how prior to 1914 Alberta's towns and cities borrowed to invest in infrastructure, paving roads, laying street railway tracks, installing sewers and improving outlying areas in anticipation of strong population growth and population sizes that did not materialize until the 1940s.

Alberta's experience with local government borrowing was common to much of Canada, as noted by Brittain: "The West is not the only part of the country where one may find miles of sidewalks, pavements and water mains with no or isolated houses, the result of the unrestricted imagination of some realtor, the simplicity of some purchasers and gullibility of municipal councils" (Brittain 1934, 389; quote cited in Tassonyi 1994). Tassonyi (1994) describes how contemporary observers felt that the extensive capital expenditures could only be justified by the realization of continued large increases in population.

After World War I, Alberta's municipalities were saddled with high debt loads and tax burdens. By 1920, Alberta municipalities collectively had as much debt as the provincial government (Hanson 1952, Figure 8.23). As Canada's investment boom ended and capital markets tightened up, municipalities found borrowing more difficult. In addition, high debts and tax obligations may have further deterred investment. By the 1920s, Alberta's municipalities were paying down outstanding debt and investing little in capital projects. The high debt loads of Canadian municipalities became a larger problem when the Depression hit in 1929, which led to the collapse of the property tax base and rising needs to borrow to make relief payments and to finance required ordinary expenditures. Many municipalities went into default on their outstanding debts, leaving their respective provincial governments to assume the debt obligations.

The end of the Depression brought little relief in terms of municipal debt loads as the resumption of economic growth and the need to catch up on deferred investments from 1920 to 1945 led municipalities to once again look at debt instruments to finance capital needs. By 1950, with the high investment demand after World War II and federal credit restrictions, municipalities in Canada were borrowing in a tight capital market.

Existing high levels of municipal debts in 1950 further deterred lenders from buying municipal debt and those capital projects that did go ahead were financed by loans from provincial governments (Hanson 1952). For example, with the arrival of the oil boom in Alberta in 1947, demands for municipal infrastructure and services soared. Edmonton's population doubled from 113,000 in 1946 to 226,000 in 1956. With this growth, Edmonton's debt increased from $12.5 million in 1946 to $22 million in 1951, and $40.5 million in 1952—almost half of the level of the provincial government's debt. Edmonton looked to the provincial and federal governments for more money, but as Premier Manning "was more generous with advice than money," telling Edmontonians to "cut back," the city borrowed heavily in Toronto and New York. By 1951, however, Edmonton had hit its borrowing limit when a $15 million issue of Edmonton debentures found no buyers on the overloaded Canadian bond market.[5]

In 1939 the Rowell-Sirois Commission confirmed that changes throughout the 1930s towards greater provincial regulation of municipal borrowing powers (in particular, to assure conservative capital financing) were positive developments (Tassonyi 1994). To that end, municipalities in Canada are restricted by provincial governments in the amount of debt they can incur, the type of debentures they can issue, the length of term, the rate of interest and/or the use of debt funds (Bird and Slack). The other change that occurred as a result of the municipal debt crisis of the 1930s was the contention that municipalities should keep as close as possible to pursuing "pay-as-you-go" policies for financing capital and other expenses. Rather than borrowing, municipalities were encouraged to overtax relative to current needs to build up funds to self-finance capital projects.

Vander Ploeg (2001) describes how all western cities follow this approach. The cities build a "cushion" with their operating budgets by ensuring that their revenues grow faster than spending. By limiting capital expenditures in the short run, the excess revenues could be used to eliminate deficits, or increase surpluses, pay down debt and accumulate reserves for the future. This strategy creates a critical mass for "own-source" capital funding as new property developments in municipalities require large capital outlays, and municipalities are reluctant to go into debt and prefer to use current revenues. Development charges on developers/builders (or, ultimately, new home buyers) have become popular approaches for municipalities in Canada to finance these additions to the stock of infrastructure (Bird and Slack 1993).

The increasing importance of conditional grants from the province to municipalities under its jurisdiction and maintenance of pay-as-you-go finance principles would appear to be appropriate responses by provincial governments seeking to control their creatures. The use of conditional grants for financing capital projects in municipalities, while in one sense undermining municipal autonomy, does insulate the provinces from the financial downside of unregulated municipal decisionmaking that caused so much fiscal hardship in the 1930s. In addition, government regulation of municipal borrowing insulates taxpayers in "responsible" communities from bearing the burden of communities who borrowed "irresponsibly." From this perspective, the 1930s highlighted the financially subordinate role of municipalities to the provinces, and hence the provincial responsibility to control municipalities.

The institutional relationship between provincial governments and their subordinate local governments implicitly allocates to the provinces the responsibility of guaranteeing that municipal financial obligations will be met. Consequently, Bird and Tassonyi (2002) argue that, as a rule, Canadian provinces put tight controls on local governments by controlling access to capital markets, directing expenditures and restricting their revenues. If local governments still manage to get into financial trouble, the provincial governments can bail out the local government by adjusting municipal boundaries, taking over spending functions and, potentially, taking control of municipal finances. Provincial control of municipalities would appear to have been successful in preventing cities from running into financial difficulties. Cities in general have had conservative financing practices and have in most cases not used their full borrowing capacity. Perhaps the best evidence of this is Bird and Tassonyi's description of how municipalities learned in the 1990s that "good guys finish last"—deficit problems led provincial governments to download some of their financial problems to local governments which were seen, politically at least, to have more room to tax and borrow.

Vander Ploeg (2001) argues that Canada's cities faced serious financial crunches in the 1990s. As provinces came to rely on transfers from the more senior levels of government, senior governments reduced their support for municipal governments because of the state of their own finances. Thus, during a decade in which many cities experienced robust growth, the cost of civic services increased and the need for infrastructure grew. Local governments faced reduced operating grants and inconsistent and unpredictable funding for capital projects. In response, cities have demanded greater revenues powers, greater shares of provincial revenues from gas taxes and other sources, and fewer restrictions and less regulation on borrowing. Bird and Tassonyi (2002) note that after 1992 Ontario liberalized local government access to capital markets to encourage municipalities to meet their needs with debt. Cities in Canada did not respond to their fiscal crunches by taking on more debt, probably because the same political pressures for senior levels of government to stop borrowing were also being exerted on local governments.

THE RISE OR FALL OF THE IMPORTANCE OF LOCAL GOVERNMENT?

Before 1930, municipal government revenues and expenditures were greater than those of their creators, the provincial governments. By the end of the Depression, however, provincial government spending and revenues equalled those of the municipal governments. Today, local government expenditures in Canada amount to less than one-quarter of provincial government expenditures. The scale and scope of government activities have grown at both the local and provincial levels, but the growth has been much larger at the provincial level. Some of the growth of the provincial government's spending has come from taking over responsibilities, such as social services, from the local governments after the 1930s. But in large part, the growth has come from the emergence of a much greater role for government in our society. In effect, the provinces assumed responsibilities like social assistance when they were growing, but still small, expenditures. It was under provincial and, in some cases, federal jurisdiction that these spending responsibilities grew to be large.

Thus, the changes to local government's importance relative to the roles of the senior levels of government took place at a time when government did not have a great deal of direct involvement in the economy. With the experience of the Depression, two world wars, the rise of publicly provided health insurance, the growing demand for postsecondary education and general growth of the welfare state, the demand for government involvement in the economy has grown enormously. Much of the growth has been in functions best suited to the senior levels of government. In an analogy to models of consumer demand, the activities of local governments would be necessary goods that increase with income but not by as much as the increase in income. The activities of the provincial income have grown with the levels of incomes, hence they are more akin to luxury goods. At the same time, an examination of proportionate changes in public spending and levels of public spending do not address the qualitative changes in economic development that may have altered the role of local government.

Transportation Revolution

From the time of Confederation to World War I, railways were the dominant mode of transportation. The structure of urban networks in the railway age was such that many small- and medium-sized spatially decentralized municipalities were linked by rail. Cities and other municipalities had roads for wagons and horses and streetcars, but the travel times and costs limited the area that could be built up. For example, by 1911 the City of Calgary covered an area of less than 50 square kilometres; its current area is 722 square kilometres.[6]

Perhaps the most significant characteristic of the rail era was the relative lack of infrastructure and economic development, both of which were the responsibilities of municipalities. The senior levels of government promoted infrastructure development for the benefit of cities and smaller municipalities. Unlike the situation described for cities today by Vander Ploeg, the senior levels of government bore much of the costs of growth and the cities reaped much of the benefits through higher property values and rising incomes. To develop the western grain economy, the federal government promoted the construction of three transcontinental railways. The provincial governments promoted railways in their own provinces to open up agricultural and resource hinterlands. The cities and municipalities that would provide the good and services to the rural population benefited from these investments. Municipal cost burdens from these investments were low as senior levels of government promoted the projects and subsidies were used, in particular loan guarantees, for private interests to build and operate the railroads. Thus, if the railway was profitable, government expenditures on these projects were not expected. As the 1920s showed, however, many railway projects were not successful (including two of the transcontinental railway projects). The federal and provincial governments then inherited some major spending headaches as the loan guarantees were exercised.

With the coming of the automobile era, infrastructure needs changed and so did the roles of local and senior levels of government. Unlike the privately built railroads, highways and roads were built and maintained directly by the three levels of government. One advantage compared to railways was that, for budgeting, the expenses were accounted for from the outset and not probabilistically as they were for railway loan guarantees. Automobiles also changed the structure of the urban/municipal network. Urban sprawl afforded by low-cost, and relatively fast, transportation pushed out the feasible limits for commuters. Indeed, the feasible limits for commuting now extend well beyond the established corporate limits of cities in Canada, creating the problem of people working in the cities but not paying taxes to support the infrastructure and services that they use. This has encouraged cities to expand their boundaries, to annex surrounding areas and communities and to rely more on user fees than property taxes.

Thus, the demands on local governments for more road infrastructure are disproportionately higher with population growth than it was during the railway era. Further, urban sprawl creates new challenges for providing police, fire fighting and ambulance services, as well as libraries and other recreation facilities. Urban sprawl in promoting retail malls in the suburbs has posed challenges for the profitability of businesses in the downtown cores. Thus, how cities have grown since the transition from rail to road has impacted on the required scale of local government services and has caused important changes to the property tax base.

Urbanization and Growth

Another change over the last century that has increased the complexity of urban governance has been the process of urbanization itself. At the time of Confederation, when most of the statutes and structures of municipal government were established, less than 20 per cent of Canada's population lived in what were considered urban areas. By 1930, half of Canada's population lived in urban areas; by 1961 two-thirds did and today, three-quarters do. In the last half-century, the character of urbanization has changed as well, as much of the rise of the urban population is occurring in the largest cities. Bird and Slack (1993) note that by 1991, one-third of Canada's population lived in the country's three largest cities—Toronto, Montreal and Vancouver.

The urbanization of Canada's population has important implications for the changing perceptions of the ideal relationship between local and provincial governments. Historically, the interests of urban voters were dominated, and then later balanced, by the interests of rural voters. In more recent times, urban voters have the dominant voice and the provincial governments have taken on the role of protecting the interests of a declining rural population. As part of these changes, how urban voters view provincial spending on rural priorities has also changed. Perhaps as late as 1960, government spending on rural areas to promote agricultural, mineral, timber and other resource production was beneficial for the urban areas that provided the goods and services for the rural population. In other words, spending to support primary production had at least a potential benefit for urban populations. Because of this, urban voters supported speculative railway projects, roads and highways that were built ahead of demand.

Since 1971, economic growth has primarily been urban economic growth. The recently released Final Report of the Prime Minister's Caucus Task Force on Urban Issues, chaired by Judy Sgro, MP, shows the importance of urban areas to provincial economies. The shares of provincial GDP generated by cities are Halifax, 47 per cent; Montreal, 49; Toronto and Ottawa,

50+; Winnipeg, 67; Calgary and Edmonton, 64; Vancouver 53 (Local Government Bulletin No. 32, November 2002). From this perspective, spending in rural areas on declining resource and agricultural sectors reduces the spending available for the industrial and service sectors located in urban areas.

Even in cases like the oil and gas economy of Alberta, where production is located in rural areas, production is capital intensive. Firms and the labour supply for the oil patch are located in Calgary and Edmonton. It is not hard to see why city governments are demanding greater shares of provincial revenues and greater fiscal autonomy from the provincial governments. The provinces get the royalties and income taxes associated with urban economic activity, but the local governments get the responsibilities for accommodating the growth of the economy and population. To some extent, the relevance of the provincial government may be in question because most of the economic growth and activity in Canada today are urban growth and activity.

CONCLUSION

The changing status of local government over the last century has resulted largely from senior levels of government taking on emergent demands for public goods and services, rather than usurping the powers and responsibilities of local governments. While the complexity of local government has grown, so has the complexity of governance at senior levels. Compared to other creatures of the provincial governments, like universities, cities have a remarkable degree of autonomy and powers for raising revenues.

Over time, provincial governments have learned that they need to control their creatures, in particular, how much the creatures choose to borrow. The lesson they have yet to learn from the recent rumblings of the creatures, and the recognition of the central importance of economically healthy urban centres for contemporary growth, is that they should not forget to feed them.

Sewell's (2002) criticism of the recent federal government report on urban issues suggests that the creatures have outgrown the creators:

> While the report talks about new partnerships, the brave words are not given structures, and the expectation of change peters out quickly as the report flails around in generalities about social harmony, sustainable environment, urban revitalization, and best practices ... Nowhere can one find a statement to the effect that cities need more powers to govern themselves well, or that their tax resources are being squandered by provincial and federal governments that take from cities

far more in taxes than they return in services, leaving cities in dire financial straits.

Based on the history behind the current relationship between the provincial governments and their creatures, is it so obvious that cities should have greater powers for governance and/or a greater share of federal and provincial tax revenues? First, assuming that the necessary constitutional changes can be made, can cities credibly be responsible for all of their own debts? Even with constitutional recognition in the BNA Act, the provinces effectively had their debts backed by the federal government in the 1930s. When the provinces resorted to borrowing from the more senior level of government, the federal government imposed controls and regulations on provincial borrowing and spending. If the solution is to make the federal government, rather than the provincial governments, responsible for backing municipal debt, is that solution desirable?

Is it a good idea to give cities a greater share of government revenues? It is naïve to view the excess of taxes taken from cities to services provided to cities as "squandered" by the senior levels of government because it neglects the fact that, over the last century, the provinces have given birth to many other creatures that must also be fed from the treasury. In addition, city residents benefit from provincial spending on health care, education, economic development, the environment and other provincial responsibilities. As city residents pay local and provincial taxes, the relevant question concerns which taxes are most desirable to raise (or, alternatively, which services are more desirable to reduce). Are city residents better off with lower property taxes but higher provincial income or sales taxes? Or are they better off with higher property taxes?

Notes

I wish to thank Almos Tassonyi, Al O'Brien and Gaby Donicht for comments.

1. For example, Alberta's 1994 Municipal Government Act states that the power of the municipality is "to provide good government," to "provide services, facilities or other things that, in the opinion of the council, are necessary or desirable," and to "develop and maintain safe and viable communities" (Local Government Bulletin No. 30, September 2002).
2. Starting in 1919, Mothers' Allowance was available to widows and mothers in custody of boys under 15 and girls under 16. Municipalities were required to pay half of these costs (Hanson: 1952, 61).
3. Dominion Bureau of Statistics (1951), Highway Statistics. Statistics Canada (1976). Transport Canada (1997), Annual Report.
4. Some municipalities also used income taxes for brief periods before World War II (Gillespie 1991).
5. Ted Byfield, ed., (2001) *Leduc, Manning & the Age of Prosperity*, vol. 9, *Alberta in the 20th Century: A Journalistic History of the Province* (Edmonton: United Western Communications Ltd.), pp. 234–235.

6. This early area estimate is based on author's "eye-balling" of a map of 1911 Calgary city limits, combined with familiarity of running trails in the area. The current area is available from the City of Calgary, "Interesting Facts," available at www.calgary.ca.

References

Bird, Richard M. and N. Enid Slack (1993), *Urban Public Finance in Canada*, 2nd ed. (Toronto: John Wiley & Sons).

―――― and Almos Tassonyi (2002), "Constraining Subnational Fiscal Behaviour in Canada: Different Approaches, Similar Results?" in J. Rodden, G. Eskeland and J. Litvack, eds., *Decentralization and Hard Budget Constraints* (Cambridge: MIT Press).

Boothe, Paul and Heather Edwards (2003), *Eric J. Hanson's Financial History of Alberta: 1905–1950* (Calgary: University of Calgary Press).

Byfield, Ted, ed. (2001), *Leduc, Manning & the Age of Prosperity*, vol. 9, *Alberta in the 20th Century: A Journalistic History of the Province* (Edmonton: United Western Communications Ltd.).

Gillespie, W. Irwin (1991), *Tax, Borrow and Spend: Financing Federal Spending in Canada, 1867–1990* (Ottawa: Carleton University Press).

Perry, J. Harvey (1989), *A Fiscal History of Canada—The Postwar Years*, Canadian Tax Paper No. 85 (Canadian Tax Foundation).

Sancton, Andrew (1999), "Affidavit of Andrew Sancton: Canadian Municipal History," Supreme Court of Canada Challenge, *Citizens' Legal Challenge Inc., et al.* vs. *Attorney General of Ontario*.

Sewell, John (2002), Local Government Bulletin No. 32, November 2002.

Struthers, James (1983), *No Fault of Their Own: Unemployment and the Canadian Welfare State 1914–1941* (Toronto: University of Toronto Press).

―――― (1994), *The Limits of Affluence: Welfare in Ontario 1920–1970* (Toronto: University of Toronto Press).

Tassonyi, Almos (1994), *Municipal Debt Limits and Supervision: The 1930s and 1990s in Ontario*, Queen's University School of Policy Studies, Discussion Paper 94–12.

Vander Ploeg, Casey (2001), *Dollars and Sense: Big City Finances in the West, 1990–2000*, Canada West Foundation, Report 2001–12.

―――― (2002), *Framing a Fiscal Fix-Up: Options for Strengthening the Finances of Western Canada's Big Cities*, Canada West Foundation, Report 2002–01.

Comments on "An Historical Perspective"

ALLISON D. O'BRIEN

J.C. HERBERT EMERY'S ESSAY PROVIDES a very useful framework for examining optimal ways to finance Canadian cities in the future. He identifies three key questions:

1) Is it obvious that cities should have greater powers for governance and/or a greater share of public revenue?
2) Can cities credibly be responsible for significant debt?
3) And critically, are city residents better off with lower property taxes but higher provincial income or sales taxes?

Almost in passing, Emery raises the fundamental issue of whether provincial governments remain relevant given that urban growth accounts for the bulk of both our economic and demographic growth in Canada. Our views on this subject will in considerable measure determine our response to the first question, respecting the need for enhanced fiscal and governance powers for Canadian and Alberta cities.

Emery concludes that the changing status of local government has resulted from senior governments taking on emergent demands for public goods—he suggests an analogy to consumer demand for necessary versus luxury goods. He does not address the question of whether senior governments are in fact the most appropriate administrative bodies to assume responsibility for delivering these emerging public "luxury goods."

Provincial efforts to "regionalize" the delivery of social services—particularly education, health care and children's and disabled services in this province—seem to me to have enjoyed notably less success than has the municipal model with its accompanying fiscal and political accountability.

On the second question respecting municipal responsibility for debt, it would be useful to see more discussion of the role of the Alberta Municipal Finance Corporation, and particularly a comparison with a body such as the BC Municipal Finance Authority which borrows on the full credit of the province-wide property tax base.

On the final question respecting the relative role of property taxation, Emery's apparent acceptance of the status quo respecting responsibility for social services leads almost inevitably to the conclusion that property taxes remain the best and most practical basis for funding municipal services, and to the rejection of "immodest proposals" for the financing of cities, such as the sales tax/business value-added tax proposals outlined in the Kneebone and McKenzie article. I support what appears to be Emery's bias—the greatest problem with financing cities through property taxation is the continuing denigration of the tax by provincial and municipal politicians alike, with the concomitant lack of attention to improving the design and administration of the property tax base.

Emery's article does not address one very important dimension of this issue, namely the role of property taxation in school financing. There are two key dimensions to school property taxation. The first is the absolute burden of school taxation, which has grown inexorably throughout Alberta's history, but with periodic reforms such as the introduction of the School Foundation Program, the removal of the provincial residential tax in the early 1970s, and the elimination of school boards' supplementary requisition powers in 1994, providing municipalities periodically with significantly enhanced "tax room" in the property tax field.

Equally important is the role that provincial school financing has played in effectively equalizing the property tax base. If more property tax room is to be made available to cities through the gradual elimination of education funding from property taxes, it will be essential to establish an explicit provincial program for equalization of municipal property tax capacity to replace the implicit equalization historically delivered through the education funding and grant system.

In the absence of such a system and of greater attention to property tax design, particularly to taxation of business property, the demand by cities for alternative sources of funding such as payroll or consumption taxes may well be irresistible.

HARRY M. KITCHEN — Financing Cities and Fiscal Sustainability

MORE THAN 80 PER CENT OF CANADA'S POPULATION is concentrated in cities and city-centred regions. In fact, it has been estimated that Canada's six largest cities have generated almost two-thirds of Canada's new jobs, well beyond their 46 per cent share of national employment (*National Post*, 2001). Further, it is this activity that has driven the provincial economies and subsequently, the national economy (Conference Board, 2001; The Prime Minister's Task Force, 2002).

City regions are places where capital, workers, institutions and infrastructure (hard and soft) come together to provide the foundations for successful economic activity. Businesses locate in cities and city-regions where they have access to a highly qualified workforce (knowledge workers), as well as access to business services, transportation and communications networks. City governments, in providing goods and services, have an important role to play in attracting and retaining businesses. The provision of local public goods and services affects the quality of life and influences where workers will live and where businesses will locate. The quality of the education system, cultural and recreational facilities, safety, transportation and the range of housing choices are important factors.

In the future, cities will face an increasing range of problems and challenges. While solutions as to what cities should do and how they should finance their services to cope with current and future challenges is neither conclusive nor obvious, there are some changes that should be implemented. These are discussed in this essay following a brief interprovincial comparison of the current level and recent growth in municipal expenditures and revenues in Canada, with special attention directed to the municipal sector in Alberta.

INTERPROVINCIAL COMPARISONS OF EXPENDITURES AND REVENUES

Although there are no uniform and consistent data permitting an interprovincial comparison of city revenues and expenditures alone, there are aggregated data for the municipal sector (cities, towns, villages, townships, counties, regions and districts) by province. Given the importance of cities and large urban areas in each province, the aggregated provincial data are dominated by the pattern in cities and large urban areas. Hence, reference to these data provides a basis for making interprovincial fiscal comparisons of cities in terms of where they have come from, where they are and what they ought to do or be permitted to do in the future if they are to remain fiscally sustainable.

Expenditures

Table 1 draws upon three municipal expenditure measures to illustrate the size of the municipal sector in Canada over the period from 1988 to 2001. Per capita expenditures are a measure of the level of municipal spending in each province. Expenditures as a per cent of gross domestic provincial product (GDPP) reflect the relative importance of each of these sectors in the overall level of economic activity within a province. Municipal spending as a per cent of consolidated provincial/municipal spending serves as a measure of the size of the municipal sector in the provincial/municipal government universe.

Per capita expenditures ranged from a low of $379 in Prince Edward Island to a high of $1,951 in Ontario in 2001 (column 3 of Table 1). Alberta was the second-highest province at $1,579, slightly above the Canadian average of $1,546. Interprovincial differences in these figures may be attributed to a combination of things, including higher servicing costs in some areas, greater municipal needs in the more highly urbanized provinces and different municipal expenditure responsibilities from province to province. From 1988 to 2001, per capita expenditures increased the most in Ontario (by $770) and British Columbia (by $456). The increase in Alberta was $273, well below the Canadian average increase of $511.

When municipal spending as a per cent of GDPP is observed, it amounts to 4.6 per cent for all of Canada in 1988 and 4.5 per cent in 2001 (columns 4 and 5). When these percentages are compared across provinces, Ontario and British Columbia are the only provinces to record an increase in the relative importance of the municipal sector. The largest proportionate decrease was noted in Alberta.

Finally, when municipal spending as a per cent of consolidated provincial/municipal spending is observed for all of Canada, it was 16.7 per cent of the total in 1988–89 and 17.3 per cent in 2001–2002. This increase in the relative importance of the municipal sector was attributed almost solely to the growth in Ontario, where municipal spending grew from 20.1 per cent of the provincial-local total in 1988–89 to 23.5 per cent in 2001–2002. New Brunswick was the only other province where the municipal sector grew in relative importance, although the increase was marginal. Municipal spending elsewhere decreased in relative importance with the largest proportionate declines occurring in Nova Scotia, Manitoba and Alberta.

TABLE 1: **Municipal Expenditures: 1988 and 2001**

Province	1988 per capita	2001 per capita	1988 % of GDPP	2001 % of GDPP	1988/89 % of provincial-local total	2001/02 % of provincial-local total
(1)	(2)	(3)	(4)	(5)	(6)	(7)
	$	$	%	%	%	%
Newfoundland	563	767	4.0	2.9	9.2	8.0
Prince Edward Is.	252	379	1.8	1.5	4.5	4.3
Nova Scotia	865	1,061	4.5	4.0	15.3	13.1
New Brunswick	551	864	3.3	3.2	10.0	10.1
Quebec	1,002	1,341	4.9	4.3	15.3	13.7
Ontario	1,181	1,951	4.6	5.3	20.1	23.5
Manitoba	871	1,091	4.5	3.6	13.8	11.7
Saskatchewan	814	1,143	4.5	3.5	12.3	12.2
Alberta	1,306	1,579	5.2	3.2	17.9	16.0
British Columbia	830	1,286	3.8	4.0	15.4	14.5
Average	1,035	1,546	4.6	4.5	16.7	17.3

Notes: Columns 2 and 3 are obtained by dividing total municipal expenditures by population for 1988 and 2001, respectively. Columns 4 and 5 record municipal expenditures as a per cent of gross domestic provincial product (an estimate of economic activity in each province) for 1988 and 2001, respectively. Columns 6 and 7 illustrate municipal government expenditures as a percent of consolidated provincial-local expenditures for the fiscal year 1988–89 and 2001–2002, respectively.

1988 is the first year for which data, over this period, are available in a uniform and consistent manner. 2001 data are estimates.

The average includes all provinces and territories.

Source: Calculated from Statistics Canada data, Financial Management Systems (FMS), mimeograph, June 2002. 2001 data are estimates.

When the municipal sector in Alberta is compared with the rest of Canada, as it is in Table 2, the following may be noted:

- In 2001, per capita spending in Alberta was $1,579 while in the rest of Canada, on average, it was $1,474.
- The difference between per capita municipal expenditures in Alberta and the rest of Canada narrowed from 1988 to 2001. In the former year, Alberta was almost $300 higher ($1,306 compared with $1,008)

TABLE 2: **Municipal Expenditures and Their Distribution, 1988 and 2001**

	1988		2001	
	Alberta	Average for rest of Canada	Alberta	Average for rest of Canada
Per capita expenditures:				
Current dollars	$1,306	$1,008	$1,579	$1,474
Constant 2001 dollars	$1,850	$1,383	$1,579	$1,474
Percentage growth, 1988 to 2001:				
Current dollars	–	–	20.9%	46.2%
Constant 2001 dollars	–	–	–14.6%	6.6%
Distribution of spending (per cent):	%	%	%	%
General administration	8.0	10.2	12.2	10.2
Protection	11.8	15.3	14.3	15.2
Transportation	29.2	21.4	28.3	20.7
Health	1.2	2.1	1.6	2.3
Social services	1.9	8.1	1.6	13.8
Education	0.0	0.1	0.3	0.4
Resource conservation	2.7	2.0	3.4	1.9
Environment	11.8	15.0	13.9	14.5
Recreation/culture	13.3	11.5	13.8	11.3
Housing	0.3	2.0	0.7	3.5
Regional planning	2.5	2.0	3.0	1.1
Debt charges	17.4	8.5	7.1	4.7
Other	0.0	1.8	0.0	0.4
Total	100.0	100.0	100.0	100.0

Note: The average for the rest of Canada excludes Alberta.
Source: Calculated from Financial Management Series data, Statistics Canada, 2002.

and in the latter year, slightly more than $100 higher ($1,579 compared with $1,474).

- Alberta's per capita expenditures increased by almost 21 per cent in current dollars and fell by almost 15 per cent in constant dollars (2001) over the period from 1988 to 2001. For the rest of Canada, the corresponding change was an increase in both current and constant dollars—by 46 per cent and almost 7 per cent, respectively.

- Expenditures on transportation (roads, streets, snow removal, public transit), protection (police and fire) and environmental services (water, sewage, solid waste collection and disposal) accounted for more than 56 per cent of all municipal spending in Alberta and slightly more than 50 per cent in the rest of Canada.
- Debt charges (for capital projects only because municipalities are not permitted to borrow for budgeted operating deficits) for Alberta accounted for 7 per cent of municipal spending in 2001 (down from 17 per cent in 1988) and for less than 5 per cent in the rest of Canada (down from 8.5 per cent in 2001). Municipal governments in Alberta retired more debt over this period when compared with other provinces.
- Expenditures on recreation and cultural services accounted for almost 14 per cent of municipal spending in Alberta, about 1.5 percentage points higher than for the rest of Canada.

Revenues

Since municipalities are not permitted to budget for operating deficits, annual operating expenditures are intended to equal annual revenues. Municipal revenues consist of grants and funds generated from own sources, including property taxes, user fees, investment income and small sums coming from a collection of amusement taxes, licences and permits, and fines and penalties. Table 3 indicates the relative importance of these revenues for the municipal sector in Alberta and the rest of Canada for 1988 and 2001. In particular:

- Own-source revenues in Alberta accounted for 84.1 per cent of municipal revenue in 2001, slightly higher than the 82.9 per cent for the rest of Canada.
- Own-source revenues increased in relative importance over the period from 1988 to 2001, from 78 per cent of all municipal revenue in Alberta in 1988 to 84.1 per cent in 2001. For the rest of Canada, the comparable increase was from 76.9 per cent to 82.9 per cent.
- Grants decreased in relative importance over this period, from 22 per cent of municipal revenue in 1988 to 15.9 per cent in 2001. For the rest of Canada, grants declined from 23.1 per cent of all municipal revenue to 17.1 per cent.
- Property taxes per capita for municipalities, the province, and school boards combined in Alberta were lower ($1,185) than those for the rest of Canada ($1,329) in 2001 and their percentage increase in Alberta over the period from 1988 to 2001 was lower—almost 46 per cent compared with 67 per cent.
- Property taxes per capita for municipal services alone in Alberta were lower than those for the rest of Canada in both 1988 and 2001.

TABLE 3: **Municipal Revenue Sources and their distribution, 1988 and 2001**

	1988		2001	
	Alberta	Average for rest of Canada	Alberta	Average for rest of Canada
Per capita property taxes for:	$	$	$	$
Municipal services	463	493	773	791
Provincial services	64	40	353	262
School boards	286	262	59	276
Total	813	795	1,185	1,329
Percentage growth, 1988 to 2001:			%	%
Municipal services	–	–	67.0	60.4
Provincial services	–	–	large	large
School boards	–	–	–79.4	5.3
Total			45.6	67.2
Municipal revenue sources (percentage distribution):	%	%	%	%
Property taxes	36.3	50.2	44.4	53.2
Other taxes	1.0	1.5	1.6	1.3
User fees	26.5	19.1	26.1	22.6
Investment income	12.8	5.1	10.3	4.2
Other	1.4	1.0	1.6	1.6
Total of own-source revenue	78.0	76.9	84.1	82.9
Unconditional grants	6.8	5.7	0.9	2.6
Conditional grants	15.2	17.4	15.0	14.5
Total grants	22.0	23.1	15.9	17.1
Total revenue	100.0	100.0	100.0	100.0

Note: The average for the rest of Canada excludes Alberta.
Source: Calculated from Financial Management Series data, Statistics Canada, 2002.

- Property taxes for municipal services in Alberta accounted for 44 per cent of all municipal revenues in 2001 (up from 36 per cent in 1988), while they accounted for 53 per cent in the rest of Canada (up from 50 per cent in 1988).
- In Alberta, user fees accounted for more than 26 per cent of all municipal revenue in 2001 (26.5 per cent in 1988), whereas for the rest of Canada they accounted for almost 23 per cent (up from 19.1 per cent in 1988).
- Investment income in Alberta accounted for more than 10 per cent of municipal revenue in 2001—for the rest of Canada, it accounted for slightly more than 4 per cent.

In summary, the reduction in the relative importance of grants over the past decade has led to a corresponding increase in reliance on own-source revenues, exclusively property taxes in Alberta, and a combination of property taxes and user fees in the rest of Canada.

FISCAL SUSTAINABILITY OF CANADIAN CITIES

The fiscal environment in which municipalities operate has changed over the past decade. Provincial grants have declined in relative importance, leading to a perception in the minds of many officials that the municipal sector will not be able to meet its expenditure commitments. Additional funding responsibilities have been transferred to municipalities and provincial governments are generally reluctant to give municipalities access to additional tax sources to fund local services (Kitchen, 2002a, chap. 2).

Many cities now face problems created by a deteriorating infrastructure and the need to replace or rehabilitate much of it, city centres that have degenerated and need to be revitalized, urban sprawl that has increased the cost of providing local services and led to inequities and inefficiencies in funding these services, and the importance of remediating and redeveloping "brownfield" sites and infilling to meet the objectives of "smart growth" policies (Onyschuk, Kovacevic, and Nikolakakos, 2001).

The combination of this new fiscal environment (Kitchen, 2000) and the growing importance of cities and urban-centred regions in an increasingly competitive global economy raises the question of whether or not cities are fiscally sustainable and whether they will be sustainable in the future. As a necessary condition for sustainability, cities must have adequate fiscal tools or levers to fund required municipal programs and needs. Furthermore, to thrive financially, municipalities must have the capacity to generate sufficient revenues to meet their current and future expenditure needs, obligations and commitments. This is impacted by at least three factors:

1. *The cyclical sensitivity of municipal funding responsibilities*: Do expenditure programs vary with the growth or slowdown in economic activity (i.e., social services, social housing, recreational programs, police and fire protection)?
2. *The capacity of the local revenue base and local taxes to keep pace with expenditure responsibilities*: Is there enough revenue elasticity in the local tax base to permit revenues to rise and fall with expenditure requirements?
3. *The ability of municipalities to control their own destinies*: Do municipalities have sufficient control over their expenditure responsibilities and revenue sources to meet changing fiscal circumstances?

At the Moment?

Currently, most cities appear to be meeting their expenditure responsibilities with current revenue sources and are, one could argue, fiscally sustainable. This, however, is at a time when the economy has come through a sustained period of growth with low unemployment. In many municipalities, especially larger cities, growth in the property tax base over the past few years has been sufficient to meet ongoing expenditure requirements without noticeable property tax increases. This has generated relatively small property tax rate increases, often less than the rate of inflation (Kitchen, 2002b).

Where property tax rates have increased, the issue of fiscal sustainability goes hand in hand with the question of whether or not there is an acceptable threshold or maximum tax rate or tax level that can be implemented. This is frequently followed by the assertion that the property tax has insufficient revenue-generating capacity to meet increased expenditure needs. In short, there is no definitive way in which one can determine this, just as there is no solid evidence to suggest that there is less revenue-generating capacity in the municipal property tax than in provincial taxes. Property tax rates can be increased and there may be solid arguments for doing so.

To gain some insight into the extent to which municipal property taxes have changed vis-à-vis provincial income and sales taxes over the past 30 years, the reader is referred to Table 4. In particular, the following may be noted: Municipal property taxes declined in relative importance in all provinces except two with the largest decline occurring in Saskatchewan, Manitoba, Alberta and British Columbia; provincial income taxes, by comparison, increased in relative importance in every province with the lowest increase occurring in Alberta; and provincial consumption-based tax revenue also increased in relative importance in every province except for two.

While these numbers do not, by themselves, support the case for higher property taxes, they do suggest that property taxes as a per cent of a common base have grown more slowly than provincial income taxes or

TABLE 4: **A Comparison of Municipal Property Tax Revenue, Provincial Income Tax Revenues, and Provincial Consumption Tax Revenues as a Percent of GDPP: 1971–72 and 2001–2002**

Province	1971–72			2001–2002		
	Municipal property taxes	Provincial income taxes	Provincial consumption taxes	Municipal property taxes	Provincial income taxes	Provincial consumption taxes
	%	%	%	%	%	%
Newfoundland	1.0	2.8	6.0	1.5	4.9	6.6
Prince Edward Is.	3.0	2.3	7.4	1.1	5.2	7.1
Nova Scotia	3.7	3.0	5.0	2.9	5.9	6.1
New Brunswick	0.8	3.4	5.6	1.7	5.4	5.5
Quebec	3.7	5.6	4.6	2.7	8.5	5.2
Ontario	4.1	3.4	3.2	2.5	5.9	4.8
Manitoba	4.0	3.9	3.5	1.7	5.8	5.2
Saskatchewan	4.8	1.8	4.0	1.8	4.3	5.0
Alberta	3.7	3.3	1.3	1.6	4.3	1.8
British Columbia	4.0	3.4	3.7	1.9	5.4	4.7
Prov. average	3.8	3.9	3.7	2.3	6.1	4.5

Source: All federal income and consumption tax revenues are excluded from the calculations in this table. Property taxation refers to municipal taxes. Provincial income taxes include personal and corporate income taxes. Provincial consumption taxes include retail sales taxes, motive fuel taxes, alcohol and tobacco taxes. Data were taken from Statistics Canada, Public Finance Historical Data 1965/66–1991/91, Catalogue 68-512 Occasional; and from data provided by Statistics Canada, Financial Management Systems (FMS), June 2002.

provincial consumption-tax revenues. The high visibility of the property tax, a perception that it is highly regressive, and concern over a possible taxpayers' revolt have all contributed to a resistance by municipal governments to use it more extensively. This information also suggests that municipalities are fiscally sustainable at the present time.

In the Future?
Will cities be fiscally sustainable in the future? They might be, but they might not be. It will depend on the extent to which the local tax (property) base grows, the extent to which cities assume increasing expenditure responsibilities (either through provincial offloading or voluntarily to meet

local needs or desires) given their increasingly important role in the competitive global economy, the extent to which local politicians are willing to raise property tax rates or extend user fees to finance needed local services, and the availability of provincial grants.

Regardless of what happens, cities will face a more challenging future than anything experienced in the recent past. To improve their capacity for meeting these challenges, to strengthen their resolve to be fiscally sustainable and to allocate their resources in a more economically (allocatively) efficient manner, a number of fiscal changes should be initiated. Some could be introduced without provincial approval. Others would require provincial approval and implementation. Furthermore, some of these changes apply to the financing of day-to-day services while others apply to financing infrastructure. These changes are discussed below.

Fiscal Changes Initiated by Municipalities

Changes over which municipalities have control include changing the current structure and application of property taxes and user fees.

Property Taxes. The current practice of imposing higher tax rates on non-residential (commercial and industrial) properties vis-à-vis single-unit residential properties, either through the application of higher assessment to market-value ratios with a constant tax rate or through the application of differentially higher tax rates (Kitchen 2002a, chap. 5), has the potential for misallocating municipal resources, being less accountable than it should be and generally unfair in its impact on taxpayers. Failure to correlate benefits from municipal services, as reflected in differences in effective property tax rates, with the extra cost of providing these services, has the potential for generating a level of output that is not optimal or allocatively efficient (Kitchen, 2000; Kitchen and Slack, 1993; KPMG, 1995). Overspending leads to higher taxes, making it more difficult for municipalities to be fiscally sustainable and competitive in the global economy.

The overtaxation of commercial and industrial property creates further problems because the amount by which the tax exceeds the cost of municipal services consumed is an annual fixed cost of doing business—it must be paid regardless of whether a profit is made or a loss incurred. This fixed-cost component has the potential to create distortions and allocative inefficiencies that could lead to a lower level of economic activity than would otherwise exist (Department of Finance, 1997). This overtaxation is an important concern for Canada because of its heavy reliance on exports and resources and its exposure to world markets.

To reverse the practice of overtaxing nonresidential properties and to set property tax rates to capture more accurately benefits received, greater use should be made of variable tax rates designed to capture cost differences across properties, property types and municipalities or neighbourhoods within municipalities (Slack, 1991). As well, or alternatively, and as is done in some municipalities, this variation could be captured through a judicious use of special assessment or benefiting area charges on properties in receipt of more costly municipal services.

User Fees. Current reliance on user fees should also be altered and expanded to improve efficiency, accountability and fairness in funding municipal services. Ultimately, the objective in setting fees should be to establish a clear link between services received and fees paid. This should be relatively easy for water and sewers, public transit, public recreation, libraries, solid waste collection and disposal, where pricing structures could take into consideration cost differentials attributed to economies of scale, capacity constraints, differential demand in peak and nonpeak periods, when second-best circumstances are prevalent and when externalities exist (Bird, 2001; Bird and Tsiopoulos, 1997; Kitchen, 1997; and Kitchen, 2000).

Current practice in setting user fees, however, almost always deviates from that which is fair, efficient and accountable. The tendency is to set fees to generate revenue, rather than to direct resources to their most efficient use. Refusal to introduce efficiency considerations (price equals marginal cost) into the pricing structure, or to entertain in any serious fashion suggestions for expanding the role for user fees, has been defended on grounds that they are regressive. This claim, however, is about as relevant as the claim that milk prices and movie tickets are regressive. Failure to price properly has created a good deal of unplanned and implicit redistribution, much of which would be unacceptable if it were made explicit. As an example, the tendency to charge a fixed price for water, regardless of quantity consumed, on the premise that fixed-income earners (poor and seniors) cannot afford to pay, provides an implicit subsidy for higher-income households with larger lawns to water and more cars to wash.

Fiscal Changes Initiated by Provinces

There are a number of changes that provincial governments could initiate to improve the fiscal viability and sustainability of municipalities. These include the transfer to the province of funding responsibilities for certain types of expenditures—those that are mainly income distributional. At the same time, not only is it impractical and unreasonable to expect cities to fund their increased spending responsibilities and requirements from a single tax, it is almost certain to be economically inefficient and unfair.

The implementation of additional taxes would offer a number of advantages. First, any single tax like the property tax is almost certain in its application to create local distortions, some of which could be offset, in all likelihood, if municipalities were permitted access to additional taxes.

Second, these would permit municipalities to achieve a broader distribution of the local tax burden among those who benefit from municipal services—residents, commuters and visitors. Third, it would make the local tax structure more flexible, thus permitting it to be tailored to fit local conditions and circumstances. Fourth, it could increase the revenue elasticity of the local tax base and allow it to adapt more easily to rising costs and service demands. Fifth, it could add additional revenue while avoiding large increases in property tax rates. Politically, this is attractive given the extent to which increases in property taxes are severely criticized by local taxpayers.

The next question is which tax or which taxes? Possible options include the income tax and consumption-based taxes (general sales tax, hotel and motel occupancy tax and fuel tax). Furthermore, these options should be viewed as supplementary to the property tax and not as substitutes for it.

Income Taxes. While cities in Canada are not permitted direct access to income taxes, some form of city income tax exists in approximately half of the OECD countries (Kitchen 2002b). In most jurisdictions, the tax is administered and collected by a senior level of government with revenues refunded to cities. In a few countries, cities have independent control—sometimes over the rate but not the base, other times over both the rate and base.

As with most potential taxes, there are two administrative alternatives. First, cities could "piggy-back" onto existing provincial income taxes by adding additional percentage points to the provincial income tax base, or they could operate their own tax system although administration costs would likely preclude this option. If cities are permitted to set their own tax rate(s), piggy-backing will give them flexibility and independence in tax policy decisions, although not as much as they would have if they set both the rate and base, yet more than they would have if a senior level of government set the rate. Where cities set their own tax rates, local accountability will be enhanced.

Although supporters of direct municipal access to income taxation have been around for some time, there are drawbacks that may make it less desirable than giving municipalities access to one or more consumption-based taxes. First, the federal and provincial governments in Canada have recently lowered personal and corporate income-tax rates to permit Canadian businesses to remain competitive (or become more competitive) internationally. If municipalities are permitted direct access to income taxation, higher tax rates could offset, or partially offset, federal and provincial initiatives and make it more difficult for businesses to compete. Second, the current practice in many developed countries, supported by most of the economic literature, is to lower reliance on income taxation and increase reliance on consumption-based taxes.

Consumption-based Taxes. There are three consumption-based taxes that are candidates. A general city sales tax, currently not permitted in Canada, is one possibility. This is used in a number of U.S. and European cities. Like the local income tax, it could be piggy-backed onto the existing federal or provincial sales taxes or, alternatively, each municipality could set up its own tax system. Piggy-backing, through the application of additional percentage points determined by city council, would be less costly to administer and would give the municipality some flexibility and autonomy.

A hotel and motel occupancy tax is another possibility (Kneebone and McKenzie, 2003), although it is currently not permitted in most provinces (British Columbia is an exception). Where occupancy or room taxes are used, they are piggy-backed onto the provincial tax and the revenue is collected by the province and returned to the municipality.

A municipal fuel tax is an obvious candidate. While many U.S. cities levy fuel taxes, only a handful of Canadian cities have access to fuel taxes. In the Greater Vancouver Regional District, revenue from an 11 cents per litre tax is used for transit and transportation services. Similarly, Victoria and Montreal also get fuel-tax revenue for transit services. Calgary and Edmonton now share in fuel-tax revenues through the provincial dedication of 5 cents per litre. None of these cities, however, has any say in the tax rate—it is determined solely by the province that collects the revenue and transfers it to the cities.

Where fuel taxes are used, their revenues are often earmarked (Bird, 1997) for local roads and public transit. A fuel tax is an efficient tax because fuel consumption is relatively unresponsive to price changes (Kneebone and McKenzie, 2003), and cities are unlikely to lose much tax revenue from consumers travelling to other jurisdictions to avoid higher tax rates—the time-cost of travel to avoid higher taxes minimizes the incentive for crossborder shopping. Furthermore, if it is a problem, municipalities can adjust their tax rates to minimize this incentive. As a benefit-based tax, it is fair if the revenues fund operating and capital costs of public transit, roads and streets.

Fiscal Changes for Financing Infrastructure

Cities, in aggregate, have the capacity to borrow more and there are solid arguments for doing so, especially where capital projects and infrastructure benefit future generations. Long-term borrowing for capital assets has declined in the recent past and annual debt-servicing charges as a per cent of operating expenditures and own-source revenues have dropped significantly. For most cities, debt service charges are well below provincial guidelines.

A general reluctance to borrow by city officials has led to a dramatic increase in "pay-as-you-go" funding (Kitchen 2002a, chap. 9). Since interest costs are a concern for municipal officials, there are some bond options that could be introduced to lower these costs and to improve a municipality's ability to meet its future obligations and needs. These would involve provincial and federal (at least in one instance) initiatives in authorizing cities to use revenue bonds, tax-exempt bonds and to create tax-incremental financing districts. At the moment, these are permitted in the United States but not in Canada.

Revenue Bonds

Revenue bonds apply to infrastructure projects that generate a revenue stream and where the beneficiaries can be identified (such as water consumption). Their credit quality depends on the financial strength of the underlying capital project with the least risky projects being those with an adequate and predictable revenue stream.

Tax-exempt Bonds

Tax-exempt bonds are those on which the interest income is not taxed under the personal or corporate income tax. While these bonds are not yet permitted in Canada, this is about to change in Ontario. Here, legislation is being developed that will permit municipalities to issue Opportunity Bonds for financing capital infrastructure—water and sewage treatment, solid waste management, roads and bridges, and public transit—that promotes "smart growth" initiatives (Ministry of Municipal Affairs, 2002). Interest will be exempt from provincial income taxes but not from federal income taxes unless the federal government agrees to cooperate.

Tax-exempt bonds have been criticized because they are inequitable; that is, they provide more income-tax relief to higher-income taxpayers than they do to lower-income taxpayers (TD Economics, 2002). The same criticism also applies to contributions to registered retirement savings plans (RRSPs) and registered pension plans (RPPs), yet both are used extensively and supported by senior governments to achieve important social (to provide an adequate level of income for retirement and to lower government expenditures for this purpose) and economic (to encourage savings and increase the supply of funds for investment purposes) objectives. Similarly, tax-exempt bonds could contribute to important provincial and national economic objectives.

Since tax-exempt bonds lower the cost of borrowing for cities and reduce provincial and federal tax revenue, this loss will be small when compared with other tax expenditures. For example, it has been estimated that if all Canadian municipal debt in 2000 (estimated at $1.5 billion) had been issued in the form of tax-exempt bonds, income tax revenues would have fallen by $50 million in that year (City of Toronto, 2000). This is comparable to the lost income tax revenue from the federal deduction for clergy residence ($50 million in 2001) and considerably lower than the lost income tax revenue from RPP ($6.19 billion) and RRSP deductions ($7.87 billion) in 2001 (Department of Finance, 2002; Bech-Hansen, 2002).

Since cities and city-regions would benefit at the expense of the general population who must now pay higher income taxes than otherwise to make up for the shortfall in income tax revenues (TD Economics, 2002), this type of subsidization may be justified. Cities and city-regions provide benefits (and hence lower taxes) in terms of economic activity that spill over onto the general population. Tax-exempt bonds could be a way of partially internalizing the spillovers or externalities created by economic activity generated in cities. The importance of this should not be underestimated in the current climate, where cities and city-regions are working to attract new economic activity (Prime Minister's Task Force, 2002) or to retain what they have. The provision of a high-quality infrastructure is an important ingredient in affecting the ability of firms/businesses to be competitive domestically and internationally.

While assistance from provincial and federal governments could take the form of grants, there are at least two observations that should be made. First, reliance on grants weakens local accountability because of the lack of a direct link between the beneficiaries of the asset and those who bear its cost. Second, grant support has declined in the recent past and there is no evidence to suggest that this trend will be reversed. The introduction of tax-exempt bonds may partially offset these concerns and provide federal and provincial assistance to cities for infrastructure needs that may have arisen, partially as a result of federal and provincial policies. Accountability should be higher because the beneficiaries will pay the costs, although they would be lower than in the absence of tax-exempt bonds and their availability should permit cities to increase their borrowing for capital infrastructure projects that benefit the local community. Tax-exempt bonds may also be a politically acceptable way for the federal government to become involved in city matters (Bech-Hansen, 2002).

Tax Incremental Financing Districts

Growing concern over the cost of brownfield remediation and redevelopment, the expense of revitalizing blighted city centres and rehabilitating deteriorating municipal infrastructure have sparked interest, from some quarters at least, in the introduction of legislation to create tax-incremental financing districts (TIDs). These are intended to stimulate private-sector investment in urban areas that need revitalization (Slack, 2002).

They are currently used by cities in 43 states in the United States (Onyschuk et. al., 2001). In general, TIDs work as follows: For a period of time long enough to recover all costs of public funds used for redevelopment, property-tax revenue from this area is divided into two categories.

Property taxes based on pre-developed assessed values are used for general purposes. Taxes on increased assessed values arising from redevelopment are used to repay bonds that have been issued to finance public improvements in the redeveloped area. Public improvement costs include land reclamation, streets, streetlights, water and sewer lines, curbs, gutters and landscaping.

In general, supporters argue that development is financed from increases in its tax revenue and not from a subsidy from other areas of the city. These do not constitute bonusing or tax abatements. Preferential treatment is granted only in that taxes from the increased assessment are dedicated to financing public improvements in the area. Finally, they may stimulate downtown development (infilling) and brownfield remediation, thus discouraging urban sprawl and promoting the so-called smart growth (Onyschuk et. al., 2001; and Toronto Board of Trade, 2002).

TIDs have been criticized where they have accelerated development that would have occurred anyway, where they have received less public scrutiny than other public spending, and where funds have been targeted to specific areas at the expense of the periphery or overall municipal growth.

CONCLUSION

The combination of increased funding responsibilities for municipalities, lower provincial grants and corresponding increases in reliance on own-source revenues over the period from the later 1980s to 2001 has changed the fiscal environment in which municipalities now operate. This has emerged at the same time as cities and urban-centred regions have become increasingly important players in the competitive global economy. These events have brought to the forefront the importance of carefully redesigning property taxes and user fees so that municipal governments are able to establish more efficient levels of service provision and to fund these services in a fair, efficient, transparent and accountable manner. At the same time, and to meet ongoing expenditure commitments, there are solid economic and, some might say, political arguments for giving municipalities access to one or more consumption-based taxes piggy-backed onto the existing provincial taxes with rates set locally.

Changes in the current structure of property taxes and user fees, plus access to new tax sources, will make it easier for municipalities to remain fiscally sustainable and economically vibrant in financing their ongoing expenditures as they confront future challenges. At the same time, many cities face serious problems with infrastructure that is deteriorating and desperately in need of rehabilitation, replacement and expansion. Many water and sewer treatment plants are in need of enlargement or rehabilitation. Transportation and public transit systems must be improved and extended. Cultural and recreational facilities need to be renewed or created. Brownfield remediation and redevelopment must be a priority and blighted areas of cities revitalized and redeveloped. The daunting prospect of financing these needs and requirements with current funding tools and instruments is one that municipalities may have difficulty meeting. It calls for an expanded range of strategies and options including the use of revenue bonds, tax-exempt bonds and the creation of tax-incremental financing districts.

References

Bech-Hansen, John (2002), "Tax-Exempt Bonds" (Toronto: Municipal Finance Officers Association).

Bird, Richard M. (2001), "User Charges in Local Government Finance," in Mila Freire and Richard Stren, eds., *The Challenge of Urban Government: Policies and Practices* (Washington, D.C.: The World Bank).

———— and Thomas Tsiopoulos (1997), "User Charges for Public Services: Potential and Problems," *Canadian Tax Journal* 45:1.

———— (1997), "Analysis of Earmarked Taxes," *Tax Notes International*, 2096–2116.

Cohen, Michael (2001), "The Impact of the Global Economy on Cities," in Mila Freire and Richard Stren, eds., *The Challenge of Urban Government: Policies and Practices* (Washington: World Bank Institute, 2001), 5–17.

Conference Board of Canada (2001), "Metropolitan Outlook," (Ottawa).

Department of Finance (2002), Tax Expenditures and Evaluations 2001, (Ottawa: The Department).

Department of Finance (1997), Report of The Technical Committee on Business Taxation, (Ottawa, The Department).

Kitchen, Harry (2002a), Municipal Revenue and Expenditure Issues in Canada (Toronto: Canadian Tax Foundation).

———— (2002b), "Canadian Municipalities: Fiscal Trends and Sustainability," *Canadian Tax Journal* 50:1, pp. 156–180.

———— (2000), "Municipal Finance in a New Fiscal Environment," Commentary, (C.D. Howe Institute, Toronto).

———— (1997), "Pricing of Local Government Services" in Paul A.R. Hobson and France St-Hilaire, eds., *Urban Governance and Finance: A Question of Who does What* (Montreal: The Institute for Research on Public Policy), 135–68.

———— and Enid Slack (1993), Business Property Taxation, Government and Competitiveness Project, Discussion Paper no. 93–24 (Kingston, Ont.: Queen's University, School of Policy Studies).

Kneebone, Ron and Ken McKenzie (2003), "Removing the Shackles: some Modest and Immodest Proposals to Pay for Cities in Alberta," this volume.

KPMG (1995), "Study of Consumption of Tax Supported City Services," a report prepared for the City of Vancouver.

Ministry of Municipal Affairs and Housing, www:bondsandzones@gov.on.ca (Ontario: The Ministry).

National Post (January 25, 2001), "Jobs generated in largest cities."

Onyschuk, B.S., M.G. Kovacevic and P. Nikolakakos (2001), *Smart Growth in America: New Ways to Create Liveable Communities* (Toronto: Canadian Urban Institute).

Prime Minister's Caucus Task Force on Urban Issues (2002), "Canada's Urban Strategy: A Vision for the 21st Century," interim report.

Slack, Enid (2002). "Municipal Finance and The Pattern of Urban Growth," commentary (Toronto: C.D. Howe Institute).
—— (2001), "Fiscal Aspects of Alternative Methods of Governing Large Metropolitan Areas," (World Bank Institute, Washington, D.C.).
—— (1991), "Variable Mill Rates," mimeograph (Toronto: Municipal Finance Branch, Ministry of Municipal Affairs).
TD Economics (April 22, 2002), "A Choice Between Investing in Canada's Cities or Disinvesting in Canada's Future," report (Toronto: TF Bank Financial Group).
Toronto Board of Trade (2002), "Strong City: Strong Nation" (Toronto: The Board).
Toronto, City of (2000), "Issuance of Tax-Exempt Municipal Debentures," report.

EDWARD C. LeSAGE

Comments on "Financing Cities and Fiscal Sustainability"

I DO NOT INTEND TO ADDRESS THE WHOLE OF Harry M. Kitchen's article, nor will I seek to provide an economic critique of it. On the first item, I restrict my comments to three brief points and then add a little something from the outfield—I'll let you draw your own conclusions concerning the field from which these final comments are tossed. On the second point, I simply observe that I am a political scientist by training, someone who has studied local government public policy and public administration, and therefore will stick to what I know best.

The three themes of my commentary are:

1. Public finance cannot be divorced from the basic question of "who does what" within the provincial-municipal complex of roles and responsibilities.
2. The "benefit principle" has utility in providing a conceptual foundation for contemplating local public finance but cannot be advanced as the sole or even principal policy heuristic.
3. Financial reform is going to be very tough if the record of the last decade and a half is anything to go by. We will most likely need both bold proposals and a usable theory to make something happen.

The point from the outfield is, simply, that the ballyhooed crisis in financing cities may be, above all, a problem of structurally promoted weak political leadership rather than of intergovernmental fiscal relations. The Alberta Urban Municipalities Association (the AUMA) has been energetic over the past two years making my first point. Specifically, the AUMA argues that no solution to the apparent crisis in urban financing can be seriously considered until the business of "who does what" is sorted out between the province and municipalities. The point is perhaps obvious. If municipal government is limited in its roles and responsibilities—say, for example, focusing principally on services to property—then defining the taxes and other revenues sources available to and required by municipal government will be fairly straightforward.

In particular, real property taxes and selected other forms of local improvement taxes and levies will likely suffice. However, if the roles and responsibilities of municipal government are extensive and elastic, municipal requirements for varied tax and other revenue resources are unquestionably more pressing. Thus, the business of sorting out who does what between levels of government is centrally important to the discussion of financing cities and the various tax instruments and revenue sources available to urban municipalities.

Kitchen surely recognizes this point and, perhaps as a contribution to deal with the conundrum, proposes that all income "distributional" services should be the responsibility of the senior levels of government. Perhaps they should, however there are problems with such a proposal. While removing the burden of having to finance and administer income-distributional services may be easily prescribed for smaller and less urbanized municipalities (since in many provinces this would seem to be the case in any event) the same cannot be said for very large urban municipal authorities. As cities and their metropolitan regions grow in size and complexity there is increased need to contemplate the whole range of distributional policy issues in the complex suite of local urban and regional public policies. In fact, while it may be theoretically possible to contemplate income-distribution policy separately from other forms of distributive policy, the reasonableness if not the practicability of doing so is questionable.

This suggests that fiscal and administrative regimes that address such complexity should be invested in larger urban governments notwithstanding the difficulties that are associated with administering income redistribution at the urban or regional level. I suppose if pressed I would concede that the financing of income distribution could be (for present purposes) a provincial function insofar as it would be provincially funded. However, conceding this, it would seem essential to establish mechanisms that permit both flexibility and connection to local policies.

My second critique of Kitchen's article is, upon reflection, something of an extension of the first. I have no quibble that the benefit principle has considerable utility in guiding us in our examination of solutions to contemporary urban fiscal problems. Within a democratic society it is expected and reasonable that there be an equitable balance between what people pay and what they receive from their public institutions. But the matter is clearly not straightforward insofar as determining what is equitable involves someone or some way of making a valuation.

A direct route toward exercising the benefit principle is to establish market or market-like mechanisms involving the purchase of municipal services and goods. These market and market-like mechanisms provide individual purchasers and policymakers with the means to value public goods and services through (or through observing) preferential purchases. Purchases made by individual citizens provide an elegant means to effect equitable distribution of public goods and services—collective social value is expressed through the exercise of these market preferences. Kitchen's suggestion that user fees should be increased is a vote in support of this approach.

Elegance acknowledged, there is a measure of intellectual imperialism imbedded in the benefit principle discourse. This is revealed in the use of concepts such as "distortions." According to Kitchen—who is by no means alone among public economists—the practice of exacting differential tax rates, such as those often placed on commercial property, is a distortion. Judged by the benefit principle, the distortion is revealed as an inequity. It is undoubtedly true that taxing commercial property at rates that are considerably higher than those on residential property violates the benefit principle. In pronounced instances it most certainly is inequitable by one of several measures and is also something that can stultify the creation of wealth. Nonetheless, the benefit principle comes with an imbedded value supposition that seems to define equity with equal and in this it is perhaps one-eyed.

There is, of course, another device that our society uses to determine value in matters of governance and public administration—the machinery of democratic politics. Broadly speaking, where the machinery of the market and that of democratic politics differ is in the authoritative aspect of value allocation exercised by the political system and in the capacity to entertain and enforce valuation equations that are not tied to purchasing power or purchasing decisions. Politics is appropriately described as the authoritative allocation of value. Reforms seeking market solutions to urban and other government problems often do so with the strong belief that political decisionmaking (the authoritative allocation of value) is perverse and more likely than not directed by special interests. I will admit that there are perversions in democratic allocation of value but argue that the system serves us quite well in many regards.

Above all, political valuation admits to the abstract notion of a general public interest. Subsidiary notions include equity, fairness, reasonableness, obligation and compassion. The public interest is served in many ways but certainly key among them is the redistribution of wealth in ways that are defined by policymakers as appropriate and that are confirmed within the broader context of open democratic processes of governance. That defining and enabling the public interest often involves significant redistribution of wealth for beneficial social purposes is the central point here. The corollary is that political leadership often involves making authoritative allocations of value that are by their very nature economically distorting and that cannot be analyzed within a narrow benefit principle accounting.

To conclude this point, I simply note that our discussion concerning how we address the fiscal problems of Canada's cities needs to acknowledge the existence of alternative systems of valuation and, with this, concepts such as the public interest as well as the benefit principle. The powerful and highly developed logic of market valuation can be seductive, and it certainly proclaims its assuredness through the use of descriptors such as "distortion." However, its power and seductiveness promote a tendency toward unidimensionality which policymakers should seek to avoid. One person's distortions are not another's—perhaps this is the point.

My third point is briefly made. Reform of urban finance is going to be difficult. In this regard, Kitchen's proposals are welcome and useful. Notwithstanding criticisms that tax-exempt bonds are problematic for various reasons and perhaps particularly owing to their "inefficiency" in relation to other approaches, Kitchen's proposals for reform appear to be practicable, if also modest. Predicting that fiscal reform is going to be difficult is, of course, pretty easy given the reform record over the past decade. Although provincial governments have initiated significant changes in structural and selected jurisdictional matters, little has been accomplished by way of substantial financial reform. There is certainly a politics to this since provincial governments are loath to see municipalities becoming competitors in the fiscal realm.

But the difficulty of reforming urban finance may also relate to the absence of a suitable theory that aids provincial and municipal governments to define who might do what and therefore how to design a new and suited regime for financing cities. And, as a flier, I add that the absence of a suitable theory concerning functional divisions between provinces and municipalities may rest on the problem of not thinking big enough when conceiving of the place of cities in Canadian governance. Simply, "big" ideas concerning what our large cities and city regions might adopt by way of functional responsibilities need to be seriously entertained to open thinking on what might be possible within a new financial regime. By example, contemplating U.S. "home-rule" styled charters or, even German Lander-like status for our largest cities would usefully move the theoretical and practical discussion to a new place. I do not argue that such statuses should be extended to cities but do suggest that these propositions not be excuded from consideration.

And now for the promised toss from the outfield. Kitchen, along with many others at this symposium, deduces that urban municipalities can afford to tax more and to generate additional revenues through currently available means such as borrowing. Nonetheless, Kitchen notes that any effort to significantly increase local taxes would be tantamount to political suicide. Most observers of Canadian local government would agree with this assessment. Still, it is worth noting that provincial governments have taken different paths to deal with fiscal exigencies and these include, in some jurisdictions, loading the public with higher taxes.

Objective circumstances and ideology have affected the divergent policy paths taken by provinces when dealing with physical stringency issues. But so too has the character of provincial political institutions. These institutions promote strong central political leadership, policy consistency and policy stability, and the leadership's ability to articulate consistent public messages. In the matter of taxation, at least some provincial leaders have been able to sell "tough love" regimes that have included rising taxes as well as service austerity measures.

Municipal leaders have been far less able to argue the tax increase side of the tough love case. One significant reason for this is that mayors and councils do not possess the strong and consistent policy voice of their provincial counterparts. The weakness is not an accident—most Canadian municipal government is politically weak because it has been designed to be weak. Provinces have an interest in weak municipal governments—one could go on for a long time with this theme. This, however, is by no means the whole story. The civic electorate has historically feared strong civic leadership and has been conditioned to accept this weakness. As a consequence, we are saddled with a preponderance of nonpartisan councils, truly "weak mayors" and often curiously drafted ward boundaries and representation schemes (e.g., multi-member wards). Such structures prevent mayors, in particular, from possessing the political muscle and the ready congregation of political supporters in council (and outside) to pursue bold policy initiatives.

In this deliberately institutionalized semi-vacuum of civic leadership it is tough to speak convincingly to the public about the need and reasonableness of drawing more wealth from the public to achieve broadly desirable or even urgently necessary public objectives. Financing our cities might become easier if a new consensus is developed that liberates us from our unfortunate structured deficit of civic leadership.

RONALD D. KNEEBONE AND
KENNETH J. McKENZIE

Removing the Shackles

Some Modest, and Some Immodest, Proposals to Pay for Cities

INTRODUCTION

THE 1990S WAS A TUMULTUOUS DECADE FOR Canadian governments. Early in the decade, the signing of free trade agreements opened Canadian industry to new competition and forced a realignment of industry toward sectors of comparative advantage. The decision by the Bank of Canada to adopt a low-inflation target at about the same time increased borrowing costs and introduced still further adjustment costs. Finally, and perhaps in response to the impact the low-inflation target had on interest rates and debt-carrying costs, the federal and provincial governments began to make concerted efforts to eliminate their deficits and to initiate a program of debt reduction. Each of these policy choices has had an important impact on the fiscal choices and budget opportunities of local governments in Canada.

While always a problem for local governments, given their small size, the general trend toward what has been referred to as "globalization" has surely forced them to take even more seriously the impact of budgetary choices on mobile taxpayers: Toronto must compete not only with Montreal and Calgary for skilled people and industry, but increasingly, and perhaps more so, with Chicago and New York. The high interest rates that accompanied the adjustment toward price stability affected local governments directly by increasing debt-carrying costs, but also indirectly as more senior levels reacted to the increase in their own carrying-costs by cutting intergovernmental transfers.

In this article we do two things: In Section 2, we describe the budgetary choices made by local governments in Canada over the period 1988–2000. Our goal in that section is to search for common themes and common responses by local governments to pressures that have been placed on their budgets. In this way we hope to be able to extract evidence on what practitioners of local government budgeting have found to be preferred tax bases and preferred spending responsibilities.

In Section 3, we turn to a more theoretical examination of what might be the most appropriate tax design for financing local governments. Rather than simply repeat the well-known "textbook" recommendations for local government tax design (although there will certainly be some of this), this section offers some "out-of-the-box" thinking on the issue. If, as has been recently proposed, local governments are to become more important players in the Canadian federation, it is important that some new thinking be offered on the question of how that level of government should be allowed to finance expenditures.

Having said this, we are cognizant of the need to keep our feet on the ground. As such, we divide our recommendations into what we call "modest" proposals on the one hand and "immodest" proposals on the other. The overriding theme of these recommendations is that, in our view, the provincial government should remove the shackles that currently restrict the revenue-raising choices available to Alberta cities. Section 4 of the article offers a summary and some concluding comments.

STYLIZED FACTS

Our goal in this article is to offer comments on what might optimistically be called "optimal" revenue sources for Canadian localities. Recognizing that what is optimal in theory is sometimes impractical in practice, we begin our discussion with a review of local government budgets and the choices local governments have made over the recent past. Thus we are cognizant of the comment directed by Richard Bird (1999) toward public finance theorists that "scholarly and policy-advising worlds have looked at the distortions and problems arising from (certain types of) taxes, shuddered, uttered some homily such as 'don't do it,' and passed on to things of more interest. Local governments facing pressing revenue needs and few other viable revenue-raising opportunities have understandably ignored such advice."

In this section we review changes in local government budgets over the period 1988–2000. In so doing, we search for common themes that might suggest what the experiences of local governments in Canada indicate is an appropriate and practical way to finance local expenditures, the appropriate level of spending on appropriate areas of local jurisdiction, and the appropriate response to the fiscal stress cities have suffered in the form of cuts to transfers, population growth and a general intolerance of taxpayers for further tax rate increases.

Expenditures

Table 1 provides data on local expenditures by province and by functional category for 1988 and 2000. These years define the beginning and end of the Financial Management Series (FMS) produced by Statistics Canada and used throughout this section of the article. These data impose a common accounting convention on the budgets of all local governments and thus enable a fair comparison both across time and space. These data are fiscal

TABLE 1: Expenditures

(a) Share of total municipal expenditure by category and by province, 1988 and 2000

	NF		PEI		NS		NB		QU		ON		MN		SK		AB		BC		Canada	
	1988	2000	1988	2000	1988	2000	1988	2000	1988	2000	1988	2000	1988	2000	1988	2000	1988	2000	1988	2000	1988	2000
General administration	13.6	18.3	10.8	13.8	7.7	11.1	8.2	9.4	13.1	13.4	8.7	9.4	12.0	18.5	11.2	15.7	8.0	11.1	7.7	9.7	9.8	10.9
Protection	6.6	4.1	18.3	22.0	12.1	17.6	23.3	22.7	14.4	18.6	15.0	14.2	15.7	18.8	15.0	16.3	11.8	13.9	19.0	19.5	14.8	15.9
Transportation	28.0	26.1	26.1	27.5	11.3	14.7	23.6	19.4	22.5	23.5	21.6	17.4	25.4	16.8	29.3	28.4	29.2	30.6	15.3	13.6	22.3	19.9
Health	0.0	0.1	0.0	0.0	0.1	0.1	0.9	0.3	0.1	0.1	2.9	3.3	2.0	0.5	2.6	0.7	1.2	1.5	5.0	1.2	2.0	2.0
Social services	0.0	0.1	0.0	0.0	23.1	4.7	0.0	0.0	0.5	0.8	14.6	25.0	5.6	0.0	1.7	0.6	1.9	1.5	0.3	0.2	7.4	12.7
Education	0.0	0.2	0.0	0.0	13.6	15.9	0.0	0.0	0.3	0.2	0.0	0.1	0.0	0.0	0.0	0.0	0.0	0.2	0.0	0.0	0.5	0.4
Resource conservation	0.4	0.5	0.7	1.4	2.7	1.0	2.3	2.3	1.3	2.2	2.4	1.5	1.8	2.3	2.1	6.9	2.7	3.2	2.2	1.6	2.1	2.0
Environment	21.2	19.5	12.3	17.0	12.3	15.9	17.3	25.2	15.9	12.9	14.2	12.2	13.7	19.1	16.8	14.6	11.8	12.5	15.0	21.2	14.5	13.9
Recreation & culture	9.7	15.4	21.0	13.2	9.1	10.3	12.5	12.4	9.7	11.9	11.2	8.4	11.9	11.1	14.8	13.1	13.3	13.9	16.1	18.1	11.6	11.1
Housing	0.6	0.5	0.0	0.0	0.6	0.6	0.7	0.2	2.6	3.3	2.3	3.5	0.3	0.7	0.0	0.2	0.3	0.6	0.8	0.6	1.8	2.5
Regional planning	2.3	1.7	2.2	1.6	1.6	3.6	1.3	3.7	1.9	2.2	1.9	2.0	2.7	1.8	2.5	1.6	2.5	3.0	2.4	2.0	2.1	2.2
Debt charges	17.4	13.4	7.6	3.5	5.5	4.1	9.8	4.3	14.1	10.6	4.1	2.8	8.4	9.5	3.9	1.7	17.4	7.6	15.2	10.1	9.6	6.0
Other	0.2	0.1	0.9	0.0	0.2	0.5	0.0	0.1	3.7	0.2	1.2	0.2	0.4	0.8	0.1	0.2	0.0	0.5	1.0	2.4	1.6	0.5
Total	100.0	100.0	100.0	100.0	100.0	100.0	100.0	100.0	100.0	100.0	100.0	100.0	100.0	100.0	100.0	100.0	100.0	100.0	100.0	100.0	100.0	100.0

... continued

Table 1 (cont'd.)

(b) Real per capita expenditures by category and by province, 1988 and 2000

	NF		PEI		NS		NB		QU		ON		MN		SK		AB		BC		Canada	
	1988	2000	1988	2000	1988	2000	1988	2000	1988	2000	1988	2000	1988	2000	1988	2000	1988	2000	1988	2000	1988	2000
General administration	101	124	36	50	90	113	60	78	173	167	138	179	144	209	123	162	145	174	87	119	137	162
Protection	49	28	61	81	142	179	170	189	191	232	239	272	189	213	166	169	215	217	214	239	207	237
Transportation	207	177	87	101	133	150	173	161	297	293	344	333	307	191	323	295	531	478	172	167	310	295
Health	0	0	0	0	2	1	7	3	2	1	46	64	24	6	28	7	21	24	57	15	28	29
Social services	0	1	0	0	271	47	0	0	6	10	232	477	68	0	19	6	34	23	3	2	103	188
Education	0	1	0	0	159	162	0	0	4	2	0	1	0	0	0	0	0	3	0	0	6	6
Resource conservation	3	4	2	5	32	10	17	20	18	28	38	29	22	26	23	72	50	51	24	20	29	30
Environment	157	133	41	62	144	162	127	209	210	161	226	234	166	216	186	151	214	195	170	260	203	207
Recreation & culture	72	105	70	48	107	105	92	103	128	148	178	160	143	126	164	136	243	217	182	222	162	164
Housing	4	4	0	0	7	6	5	2	34	41	36	67	3	8	0	2	5	9	9	7	25	38
Regional planning	17	12	7	6	18	36	9	31	25	27	30	39	32	21	28	17	46	46	27	24	29	33
Debt charges	129	91	25	13	64	42	72	36	186	132	65	53	101	108	43	18	318	118	171	123	133	89
Other	1	0	3	0	3	5	0	1	49	3	19	4	5	9	1	2	0	8	11	29	22	8
Total	$741	$679	$334	$366	$1,172	$1,020	$733	$832	$1,323	$1,245	$1,593	$1,913	$1,205	$1,133	$1,105	$1,036	$1,823	$1,563	$1,128	$1,228	$1,394	$1,486
Program spending as a percentage of total provincial plus local government program spending	9.7%	8.5%	5.0%	5.3%	17.5%	16.6%	10.6%	11.8%	15.8%	15.4%	23.0%	27.5%	16.0%	15.1%	16.0%	15.1%	17.7%	18.4%	15.7%	15.9%	18.3%	20.0%
Average annual growth rate in real per capita total expenditures since 1988	-0.7%		0.8%		-1.2%		1.1%		-0.5%		1.5%		-0.5%		-0.5%		-1.3%		0.7%		0.5%	
Average annual growth rate in real per capita program expenditures since 1988	-0.3%		1.1%		-1.0%		1.6%		-0.2%		1.7%		-0.6%		-0.3%		-0.3%		1.2%		0.9%	

year, ending December 31, and represent the revenues and expenditures of local general government. As such they do not include the budgets of school boards. Panel (a) of Table 1 shows spending in each category as a percentage of total spending. Panel (b) shows spending by functional category in real per capita terms. These values are measured in 2000 dollars.[1]

Immediately apparent from the data on real per capita total expenditure is that local governments in Newfoundland, Prince Edward Island and New Brunswick play a significantly smaller role in providing goods and services than local governments in the other seven provinces. This is apparent not only from comparing the size of real per capita spending across provinces but also by a comparison across provinces of the share of total provincial plus local program spending done by local governments. Also noteworthy is the fact that Ontario is the only province in which there was an appreciable increase in the share of goods and services provided by local governments over the period 1988–2000.

While panels (a) and (b) also contain average values for all local governments in Canada, these data must be used with caution because of wide differences in the responsibilities of local governments. This is particularly so with respect to local government spending in the area of social services, an expenditure responsibility of minor importance in all provinces but Ontario. Local responsibility for social services was being phased out over this period in Nova Scotia, with spending falling steadily since 1994. This follows the pattern in Manitoba where local spending on social services fell steadily from a peak in 1993 to zero in 2000.

Ontario stands out as the only province in which local governments have been assigned the responsibility for a large share of spending on social services. Ontario is, as Kitchen (2000) notes, a "distinct society" in this regard. The growing share of local spending in total provincial plus local spending on programs in Ontario is almost wholly due to growth in this category. Local governments in Nova Scotia are similarly distinct in that they are the only local governments in Canada with a noticeable responsibility for spending on elementary and secondary education (remember that the numbers do not include school boards).

Local governments in Ontario spend more per capita than in any other province, averaging $1,913 per person in 2000. Local governments in Alberta, Quebec and British Columbia follow as second- to fourth-largest spenders on a per capita basis while local governments in Newfoundland and PEI spend the least. This ordering suggests that the demand for local services arising due to urbanization more than offsets savings due to economies of scale and is a key determinant of the size of local government spending. Local government spending has increased most rapidly in Ontario (driven mainly by spending on social services) and in New Brunswick (driven mainly by spending on environment) where real per capita spending has increased by an average of 1.5 per cent and 1.1 per cent annually, respectively.

On the other hand, local government spending has fallen over this period by an annual average of 1.3 per cent in Alberta (due mainly to savings on debt charges) and 1.2 per cent in Nova Scotia (due to the withdrawal from social services). Finally, it is also noteworthy that local governments in Alberta, Saskatchewan, New Brunswick and PEI used the period 1988 to 2000 to institute budgets that leaned heavily on debt reduction. This can be inferred from the fact that local governments in those provinces reduced debt charges substantially more than local governments in other provinces.[2]

Surpluses are used by local governments for debt repayment, pay-as-you-go capital financing and/or for adding to reserve funds. To the extent surpluses are used to reduce debt, annual debt charges fall. Local governments in Alberta paid an average of $318 per person in debt charges in 1988, by far the largest amount in Canada. This amount fell steadily over time both absolutely and relative to debt charges in other provinces. By 2000 debt charges were a third of what they were in 1988. In no province did local governments come close to retiring as much debt as local governments in Alberta.

Tax Revenues

Table 2 provides data on local revenues by province and by functional category for 1988 and for 2000. Panel (a) of Table 2 shows revenue in each category as a percentage of total revenue while panel (b) shows revenue in each category in real per capita terms. As we found with respect to expenditures, it is again apparent from these data that local governments in Newfoundland, PEI and New Brunswick play a significantly smaller role in those provinces than is the case of local governments in the other seven provinces.

Local government revenues have grown rapidly over the period 1988–2000 in some provinces (particularly PEI and Newfoundland) but shrunk rapidly in others (particularly Saskatchewan and Nova Scotia). The growth rate in total revenue shows the weighted influence of growth rates in own source revenues and intergovernmental transfers, two revenue categories that have moved in opposite directions over this period (the exception being Quebec). Thus local governments have been forced to engage in a substantial "re-mixing" of their revenue sources because of changes in intergovernmental transfers.

Property taxes are by far the largest source of revenue and on average raise about 50 per cent of total local government revenue. Local governments in Nova Scotia and Quebec rely significantly more on property tax revenue than local governments elsewhere, while local governments in Alberta relied least heavily on the property tax. The share of the property

TABLE 2: Revenues

(a) Share of total municipal revenue by category and by province, 1988 and 2000

	NF		PEI		NS		NB		QU		ON		MN		SK		AB		BC		Canada	
	1988	2000	1988	2000	1988	2000	1988	2000	1988	2000	1988	2000	1988	2000	1988	2000	1988	2000	1988	2000	1988	2000
Property taxes	41.9	47.1	50.0	62.4	58.0	73.0	41.7	55.7	68.8	67.3	41.7	49.8	44.5	48.5	48.1	54.5	36.3	42.7	48.0	51.7	48.7	53.6
Real property	27.9	32.8	49.5	62.1	43.4	57.1	33.1	47.9	39.0	43.6	29.4	43.9	30.5	36.7	39.3	43.9	21.4	30.9	39.9	44.6	32.5	42.5
Business taxes	9.2	9.7	0.0	0.0	6.0	6.7	0.0	0.0	7.7	9.0	4.4	0.0	3.7	4.8	1.2	0.6	4.7	4.1	0.0	0.0	4.7	2.8
Consumption & other taxes	1.9	1.2	0.5	0.5	0.6	0.2	0.5	0.5	1.0	0.3	1.3	1.3	2.2	2.2	3.9	4.5	1.0	1.3	2.5	2.6	1.4	1.3
User fees	12.6	14.6	30.7	26.7	10.8	17.2	18.9	22.2	16.5	16.9	20.0	19.6	17.7	25.7	21.4	25.7	26.5	28.3	23.7	28.9	19.9	21.3
Investment income	1.9	1.3	3.7	2.1	3.7	3.0	1.2	0.8	3.0	2.3	5.1	4.3	8.3	6.4	6.7	5.8	12.8	10.3	10.1	9.3	6.0	5.0
Other own source	0.4	0.5	1.2	1.5	0.8	0.3	0.6	0.5	2.0	2.4	0.7	0.8	1.0	0.7	1.4	1.1	1.4	1.7	0.5	0.7	1.1	1.2
Total own source	58.8	64.7	86.1	93.2	73.7	93.8	63.0	79.7	91.3	89.1	68.8	75.8	73.7	83.5	81.3	91.6	78.0	84.3	84.9	93.1	77.2	82.4
General purpose grants	18.2	5.5	12.2	3.6	4.6	2.7	26.5	12.6	0.5	0.8	7.3	3.3	7.8	8.4	10.1	5.3	6.8	1.3	4.3	1.0	5.8	2.6
Specific purpose grants	23.0	29.9	1.7	3.2	21.6	3.5	10.5	7.7	8.3	10.0	23.8	20.9	18.5	8.1	8.6	3.1	15.2	14.4	10.8	5.9	17.0	15.0
Federal	3.1	3.4	0.2	1.1	0.4	0.6	1.6	1.0	0.2	0.3	0.9	0.9	1.2	0.7	0.3	1.2	0.5	0.7	1.1	0.7	0.7	0.7
Provincial	19.9	26.5	1.5	2.1	21.2	2.9	8.9	6.7	8.1	9.8	23.0	20.1	17.3	7.4	8.2	1.9	14.7	13.7	9.7	5.2	16.3	14.3
Total grants	41.2	35.3	13.9	6.8	26.3	6.2	37.0	20.3	8.7	10.9	31.2	24.2	26.3	16.5	18.7	8.4	22.0	15.7	15.1	6.9	22.8	17.6
Total	100.0	100.0	100.0	100.0	100.0	100.0	100.0	100.0	100.0	100.0	100.0	100.0	100.0	100.0	100.0	100.0	100.0	100.0	100.0	100.0	100.0	100.0

...continued

TABLE 2 (CONT'D.)

(b) Real per capita revenues by category and by province, 1988 and 2000

	NF		PEI		NS		NB		QU		ON		MN		SK		AB		BC		Canada	
	1988	2000	1988	2000	1988	2000	1988	2000	1988	2000	1988	2000	1988	2000	1988	2000	1988	2000	1988	2000	1988	2000
Property taxes	272	352	150	249	641	730	297	439	832	876	669	891	528	537	527	535	645	707	540	598	662	777
Real property	181	246	148	248	479	571	236	378	472	568	472	785	362	406	431	431	380	512	449	516	441	616
Business taxes	60	73	0	0	66	67	0	0	93	117	70	0	44	53	13	6	83	68	0	0	63	40
Consumption & other taxes	12	9	2	2	6	2	4	4	12	4	22	23	26	24	42	44	18	21	28	30	19	18
User fees	82	109	92	106	119	172	134	175	200	220	322	351	210	285	234	252	472	468	267	334	271	308
Investment income	12	10	11	9	41	30	9	7	36	30	82	76	98	71	73	57	228	171	113	107	82	73
Other own source	3	4	4	6	8	3	5	4	24	31	11	14	12	8	15	11	24	27	6	8	15	17
Total own source	382	484	258	372	815	938	449	629	1,104	1,161	1,105	1,355	874	925	892	899	1,388	1,395	955	1,077	1,048	1,194
General purpose grants	118	41	37	14	51	27	189	99	5	11	118	58	92	93	111	52	120	22	48	11	79	38
Specific purpose grants	150	224	5	13	239	35	75	61	100	131	383	374	219	90	94	30	270	238	121	68	231	217
Federal	20	25	1	5	4	6	11	8	2	3	14	16	14	8	4	12	9	12	12	8	10	11
Provincial	129	198	4	8	235	29	63	53	98	127	369	359	205	82	90	18	261	226	109	60	222	207
Total Grants	268	264	42	27	290	62	264	160	106	142	501	433	311	183	205	82	390	259	170	79	310	255
Total	$649	$748	$300	$399	$1,106	$1,000	$713	$789	$1,210	$1,302	$1,606	$1,788	$1,185	$1,107	$1,097	$981	$1,778	$1,654	$1,124	$1,156	$1,359	$1,448
Total revenue as a percentage of total provincial plus local government revenue	8.8	9.0%	4.4%	5.3%	16.1%	14.0%	10.1%	10.0%	16.0%	14.6%	21.9%	23.6%	14.1%	13.6%	14.7%	12.3%	20.6%	14.9%	15.4%	14.6%	18.0%	17.4%
Average annual growth rate in real per capita total revenue since 1988	1.2%		2.4%		-0.8%		0.8%		0.6%		0.9%		-0.6%		-0.9%		-0.6%		0.2%		0.5%	
Average annual growth rate in real per capita own source revenue since 1988	2.0%		3.1%		1.2%		2.8%		0.4%		1.7%		0.5%		0.1%		0.0%		1.0%		1.1%	
Average annual growth rate in real per capita transfers since 1988	-0.1%		-3.6%		-12.0%		-4.1%		2.5%		-1.2%		-4.3%		-7.4%		-3.4%		-6.1%		-1.6%	

tax in total revenue has increased fairly steadily in every province but Quebec, where the share has remained more or less constant, and Ontario, where the share of the property tax increased rather precipitously from 39 per cent in 1995 to 50 per cent in 2000; an increase of $180 in real per capita terms.

Within the property-tax category, there is some heterogeneity in local taxes across provinces. Local governments in six provinces collect a business tax in addition to residential and nonresidential property taxes. Local governments in Ontario abandoned the business tax as a revenue source in 1998 and simultaneously increased the nonresidential portion of real property taxes. Local governments in Saskatchewan and Alberta, while not abandoning the business tax, chose to reduce the amount collected.

Amongst own-source revenues, user fees are generally the next largest source of revenue for local governments. Relying most heavily on user fees are local governments in BC, Alberta, PEI, Saskatchewan and Manitoba, where in 2000 user fees contributed between 26 per cent and 29 per cent of total revenues. Local governments in Newfoundland and Quebec relied least heavily on user fees in 2000. On a real per capita basis, user fees are largest in Alberta where in 2000 they averaged $468 per person, and smallest in PEI where in 2000 they averaged just $106 per capita. While the highest in Canada, user fees in Alberta have remained more or less constant in real per capita terms since 1988. On the other hand, user fees grew particularly quickly in real per capita terms over the 1988–2000 period in Nova Scotia (3.1 per cent growth per year), Manitoba (2.6 per cent) and Newfoundland (2.5 per cent).

Intergovernmental Transfers

The calculations in Table 2 show transfers to have been the most volatile revenue source for local governments over the period 1988–2000. Local governments in Quebec were the only ones in Canada to realize an increase in the share of transfers in total revenues and were the only local governments in Canada to realize an increase in transfers measured in real per capita terms. The experience of local governments in Quebec is also unique in that transfers made up such a small fraction of total revenues in 1988; just 8.7 per cent of total revenue. Between 1988 and 2000, the other provinces took steps toward the Quebec model of minimizing the reliance of local governments on intergovernmental transfers. The biggest steps have been taken by provincial governments in Nova Scotia and New Brunswick, which have cut transfers to local governments sufficient to reduce the share of total revenues accounted for by transfers by 20 and 17 percentage points respectively.[3] Nova Scotia is particularly notable in that transfers in that province went from making up 30 per cent of local revenues in 1995 to making up just 6 per cent in 2000. This marked a massive and speedy cut in local transfers in that province. No other province imposed so large a cut in transfers on its local governments.

An interesting aspect of the reduction in provincial transfers to local governments over this period is that they were disproportionately weighted toward general-purpose transfers. Manitoba and Quebec were the only provinces during this period that maintained the size of general-purpose transfers to its local governments in real per capita terms. Newfoundland, while not cutting transfers, nonetheless changed the mix away from general-purpose toward specific-purpose grants. This period, then, was one during which local governments were finding their budget flexibility severely reduced, not only by cuts to the size of transfers but also by changes to the type of transfer received. By 2000, Alberta had joined Quebec as the two provinces whose intergovernmental transfers were most heavily weighted toward specific-purpose transfers and thus provided the least flexibility to their local governments.

Table 3 offers a closer look at what has happened to intergovernmental transfers in Canada between 1988 and 2000. Two columns of figures are presented for each province. The first column presents data measuring the size of the transfers the provincial government receives from the federal government. All types of federal transfers are included: Equalization, the CHST and the predecessors to the CHST, Established Program Funding and the Canada Assistance Program. The second column of figures measures the size of provincial transfers to their local governments. In panel (a) these two sets of transfers are presented as a percentage of provincial program expenditures while in panel (b) they are presented in real per capita dollars.

Federal transfers to the provinces fell from financing an average of 21.4 per cent of provincial program expenditures in 1988 to financing an average of 17.6 per cent in 2000. Cuts in federal transfers to the provinces were accompanied by a change in the composition of transfers from specific-purpose toward general-purpose transfers.[4] This change increased the budget flexibility of provincial governments and in so doing satisfied a demand for which they lobbied the federal government long and hard. It is interesting, then, to observe the size and nature of cuts of provincial transfers to their local governments in light of the displeasure provincial governments have expressed over the size of cuts in federal transfer to them and their desire for increased budget flexibility.

Federal transfers to the Atlantic provinces, Quebec and Manitoba remained more or less constant from 1988–2000 in real per capita terms. Despite this, New Brunswick cut transfers to its own local governments more or less steadily from 1988–2000. Newfoundland and, until 2000, Manitoba left local transfers basically unchanged while PEI, Nova Scotia and Quebec, after increasing the size of local transfers up until the mid-1990s,

TABLE 3: Intergovernmental Transfers

(a) Intergovernmental transfers received as a percentage of program expenditures

	NF		PEI		NS		NB		QU		ON		MN		SK		AB		BC		Canada	
	Province	Local	Province	Local	Province	Local	Province	Local	Province	Local	Province	Local	Province	Local	Province	Local	Province	Local	Province	Local	Province	Local
1988	53.9	43.7	50.5	13.5	43.2	26.2	43.8	39.9	22.1	9.3	22.1	32.8	35.5	28.2	27.1	19.3	16.9	25.9	18.1	17.7	21.4	24.6
1989	54.9	41.1	49.0	13.6	38.7	27.0	43.4	37.3	22.6	10.2	22.6	31.2	35.2	27.9	28.0	18.7	14.6	23.9	15.7	18.7	20.9	23.9
1990	50.0	38.0	47.8	18.5	43.0	26.4	41.5	34.7	21.1	9.7	21.1	31.4	36.2	27.8	30.8	18.8	17.4	24.4	13.8	18.1	20.2	24.0
1991	48.6	37.7	43.8	15.8	41.8	27.0	38.3	34.1	19.4	9.7	19.4	35.1	36.4	28.3	27.3	17.5	15.2	23.4	12.5	15.6	18.7	25.8
1992	48.7	36.6	43.3	16.5	37.2	27.7	45.7	33.9	21.3	11.3	21.3	37.7	34.5	31.1	33.7	14.3	16.3	25.9	14.2	16.0	20.4	27.5
1993	50.4	36.8	32.1	19.0	40.8	28.0	39.7	31.8	21.2	13.8	21.2	37.6	32.2	30.4	24.8	12.7	15.5	14.9	12.2	15.4	19.5	26.8
1994	54.2	40.1	48.2	21.4	48.5	27.7	41.4	31.8	20.7	14.2	20.7	38.3	38.3	31.4	31.2	12.6	14.3	17.0	12.3	13.7	20.3	27.1
1995	51.2	44.0	44.6	13.0	47.7	30.4	40.9	29.4	22.2	15.0	22.2	38.1	37.1	30.9	22.0	12.2	13.6	17.4	11.7	16.4	20.0	27.5
1996	49.5	48.3	40.3	11.3	46.0	14.5	38.5	26.6	19.3	14.4	19.3	33.1	32.8	29.8	18.4	12.1	10.5	16.2	9.3	15.5	17.1	24.0
1997	65.5	47.3	41.2	8.7	48.3	12.9	41.9	23.4	17.6	13.8	17.6	30.1	34.2	33.5	14.1	8.7	8.8	15.0	9.2	12.1	16.1	21.9
1998	55.4	47.3	46.5	8.2	47.4	6.1	51.3	21.4	22.3	14.6	22.3	25.9	27.7	30.7	20.7	8.5	9.2	13.8	7.8	8.6	16.4	19.7
1999	51.2	44.6	44.2	7.8	44.8	6.6	43.2	21.6	18.9	12.9	18.9	24.0	33.7	29.5	24.2	8.9	10.8	18.1	11.9	49.9	17.6	23.5
2000	51.8	45.0	45.2	7.7	45.0	6.4	42.4	20.1	21.4	12.7	21.4	23.3	30.5	17.8	17.8	8.0	9.1	17.9	13.3	7.2	17.6	18.2

... continued

TABLE 3 (CONT'D.)

(b) Intergovernmental transfers received, real per capita dollars

	NF		PEI		NS		NB		QU		ON		MN		SK		AB		BC		Canada	
	Province	Local	Province	Local	Province	Local	Province	Local	Province	Local	Province	Local	Province	Local	Province	Local	Province	Local	Province	Local	Province	Local
1988	3,077	248	2,983	41	2,258	286	2,452	252	1,338	103	735	486	2,050	297	1,508	201	1,182	382	929	157	1,200	300
1989	3,233	228	3,023	40	2,269	302	2,499	238	1,332	122	721	476	2,090	295	1,751	195	1,018	366	863	172	1,185	304
1990	3,029	228	2,971	57	2,226	310	2,445	242	1,281	119	719	520	2,089	296	1,857	199	1,175	382	773	179	1,166	324
1991	2,874	212	2,668	40	2,074	381	2,197	226	1,173	111	735	618	2,153	294	1,990	166	985	336	752	155	1,112	349
1992	3,013	219	2,655	45	2,040	330	2,637	227	1,321	134	859	675	2,003	327	1,874	135	1,091	376	850	170	1,221	381
1993	2,894	215	2,381	51	1,995	337	2,255	216	1,281	164	792	662	1,814	318	1,437	108	927	211	726	163	1,114	366
1994	3,221	218	2,799	58	2,360	327	2,388	208	1,299	178	829	667	2,049	320	1,656	114	817	220	746	148	1,156	368
1995	3,027	239	2,545	37	2,371	346	2,348	210	1,359	188	804	646	1,943	343	1,119	123	716	214	691	170	1,114	368
1996	2,933	222	2,296	28	2,139	133	2,156	191	1,139	174	599	502	1,717	313	888	103	540	187	551	159	913	298
1997	3,772	239	2,309	23	2,272	124	2,334	170	1,010	162	485	456	1,829	351	702	74	457	178	535	124	848	272
1998	3,442	231	2,780	24	2,376	58	2,968	164	1,342	170	459	434	1,518	324	1,106	77	492	169	611	89	948	258
1999	3,169	238	2,764	22	2,263	59	2,643	166	1,163	143	581	424	1,973	329	1,335	81	625	241	718	554	984	318
2000	3,289	239	2,877	22	2,204	56	2,521	152	1,306	138	545	417	1,765	175	1,016	70	585	248	778	71	983	244
Rho	0.48		0.24		-0.29		-0.31		-0.09		0.86		0.04		0.73		0.90		0.05		0.65	

Notes: *Data on federal transfers to the provinces are fiscal year ending March 31st. Data on provincial transfers to local governments are calendar year. The data on transfers from the federal government to the provinces for the fiscal year ending March 31st are used to represent transfers in the previous calendar year.*

cut them thereafter. Federal transfers to the province of Ontario have fallen since 1994 and, interestingly, Ontario's transfers to its local governments have fallen by almost the same amount in real per capita terms. Saskatchewan has experienced wide swings in federal transfers mainly due to swings in the size of equalization payments caused by the province being on the cusp of "have" status. Saskatchewan's local governments have suffered a steady decline in the size of provincial transfers.

In Alberta, local governments shared in the budget-cutting exercise of the newly elected Klein government in 1993. Transfers were cut by over 40 per cent in that year and would suffer further cuts in 1998. The last two years of our sample saw a major increase in local transfers, coincident with an increase in transfers received by Alberta's provincial government. Despite a $227 real per capita increase in federal transfer receipts between 1995 and 2000, the government of British Columbia has cut on-going local transfers by $88 over the same period. A one-time transfer of about $2 billion occurred in 1999.

The last row of panel (b) in Table 3 shows the calculation of the correlation coefficient (*rho*) between transfers received by a province from the federal government and transfers local governments received from the province. Changes in the two sets of transfers are highly and positively correlated in Alberta, Ontario and Saskatchewan, suggesting that local governments in those provinces have been asked to share in the cuts imposed on the province by the federal government. Interestingly, changes in the two sets of transfers are negatively correlated in Nova Scotia and New Brunswick. Given that federal transfers to those provinces have remained more or less constant, local governments in those provinces were asked to suffer what the provincial government did not.

The idea that efforts at deficit reduction might come at the expense of intergovernmental transfers is not new, nor is it surprising.[5] Taxpayer/voters tend to identify the unpleasant consequences of transfer cuts with the receiving rather than the transferring government. From a political economy perspective then, it makes good sense for a government to cut the size of transfers, as it will pay a smaller political cost for cutting there than in areas more clearly defined in the minds of voters with their own sphere of responsibility.

The Fiscally Stressed
Deficit cutting by both federal and provincial governments, because of the frequency with which it is accomplished via reductions in intergovernmental transfers, the ease with which these cuts are passed on to ever-lower levels of government, and the frequency with which they were weighted toward cuts to general-purpose transfers, was an important source of fiscal stress for local governments over the period 1988–2000.[6] Adding to the stress of

having to respond to cuts to transfers was the fact that the cuts were often very large and very sudden.

From panel (b) of Table 3 we can identify 24 cases of transfers from a province to its local governments falling in real per capita terms by 10 per cent or more in a single year, 18 cases of cuts equal to 15 per cent or more, and 13 cases of cuts equal to 20 per cent or more in a single year. The province of Saskatchewan is notable for cutting transfers to its local governments by an amount equal to 15 per cent or more five times between 1991 and 1997. Alberta, Manitoba, British Columbia and Nova Scotia (twice) are notable for introducing cuts to real per capita transfers in excess of 40 per cent in a single year.

We noted earlier that local governments in more densely populated provinces (Ontario, Alberta, Quebec and BC) spend more on a per capita basis than local governments elsewhere. This suggests that another key source of fiscal stress for local governments is population growth: A rapid rate of population growth demands growth in expenditures to keep up with demands for local infrastructure. If this is the case, then fiscal stress faced by local governments in BC (where the rate of population growth averaged 2.2 per cent per year between 1988 and 2000), Alberta (1.7 per cent) and Ontario (1.4 per cent) has been significantly greater than elsewhere (where population grew at an average of 0.4 per cent per year).

Using the rate of population growth, along with the size and frequency of cuts to transfers received from the province, as indicators of fiscal stress for local governments, we identify local governments in the following provinces during the specified periods as being subjected to particularly high levels of fiscal stress: Ontario (from 1996–2000), British Columbia (from 1995–98), Saskatchewan (from 1991–97) and Alberta (1993–98).[7] In those provinces over those periods, population was growing by an average of 1.3 per cent per year, intergovernmental transfers where cut by an average of 33 per cent and the cuts to transfers were dominated by cuts to general-purpose transfers, thus limiting the flexibility local governments had over how to spend the shrinking transfer. The key responses of these highly stressed local governments are described in Table 4.

The most significant response of highly stressed local governments in Ontario and Alberta was to increase the real per capita amount of revenue collected from property taxes by 28 per cent and 10 per cent respectively. Local governments in BC and Saskatchewan also increased property taxes but by more modest amounts, 3 per cent and 2 per cent respectively. At the same time, however, the business-tax portion of total property-tax revenue was eliminated in Ontario and severely cut in Saskatchewan and Alberta. Local governments in British Columbia continued to avoid the use of business taxes.

TABLE 4: **Fiscal Responses of the Fiscally Stressed**

Average Response of Local Governments	Ontario (1996–2000)	Saskatchewan (1991–1997)	Alberta (1993–1998)	British Columbia (1995–1998)
Key Revenue Responses*				
Property taxes	28%	2%	10%	3%
Real property	48%	–1%	23%	5%
Business taxes	–100%	–24%	–9%	NA
User fees	8%	15%	7%	11%
Key Expenditure Responses*				
Protection	14%	–4%	–3%	2%
Transportation	12%	–1%	–14%	0%
Environment	2%	13%	–13%	9%
Recreation & culture	–13%	–16%	–9%	–4%

Note: * *Percentage change in real per capita revenue/spending during the period of fiscal stress.*

Local government in all four provinces increased user fees, the second-largest source of own-source revenues for local governments. Thus, fiscally stressed local governments reacted to that stress by shifting revenue collection toward relatively immobile taxpayers (residential property owners) and away from relatively mobile taxpayers (businesses). They also responded by increasing user fees and thus increasing the fraction of total revenues collected from those most directly benefiting from local government expenditures.

On the spending side, a common response of fiscally stressed local governments was to cut real per capita spending on recreation and culture, a functional area that might be viewed as being amongst the least crucial in the realm of local government spending responsibilities. Local government spending on transportation was reduced in Alberta. This response is consistent with the perception that fiscally stressed governments might delay investments in infrastructure. That response, however, was unique to Alberta. Fiscally stressed local governments in Ontario increased spending on transportation, while in the other provinces local governments held spending constant in real per capita terms. Similarly, spending in the functional area of environment—water purification and supply, garbage and waste collection, sewage treatment—the sort of spending, along with police and fire protection and transportation, that taxpayers most closely identify with local governments, was reduced by stressed local governments in Alberta but increased by the same percentage by similarly stressed governments in Saskatchewan.

The Bottom Line on Stylized Facts

The goal of this section was to review recent changes to local government budgets with an eye to uncovering evidence of what budgetmakers at the local level have found to be appropriate and practical ways of raising revenue and uncovering what these practitioners have found to be appropriate levels of expenditure in their jurisdiction. We have found little in the way of responses and experiences that are common to local governments in all provinces. A frequent experience over the 1988–2000 period was having to deal with rather large cuts to the size of transfers received from provincial governments (local governments in Quebec and Newfoundland were exceptions). These cuts tended to be accompanied by a change in the mix of transfers away from general-purpose grants and toward specific-purpose grants (something local governments in Newfoundland experienced even in the absence of an overall cut to transfers).

On the assumption that nothing focuses attention and exposes fundamental beliefs and principles like a high degree of budgetary stress, we turned our attention to the budgetary choices made by particularly stressed local governments in Ontario between 1996 and 2000, in Saskatchewan between 1991 and 1997, in Alberta between 1993 and 1998, and in British Columbia between 1995 and 1998. This analysis revealed that when push came to shove local governments hunkered down by cutting spending in less crucial areas, raising revenue and changing their revenue mix. In particular, fiscally stressed local governments were observed to raise taxes on immobile taxpayers, cut taxes imposed on relatively mobile taxpayers and increase taxes paid by those directly benefiting from local expenditures by increasing user fees.

SOME PROPOSALS WITH RESPECT TO LOCAL GOVERNMENT REVENUES

We interpret the findings of the previous section not only as suggesting a remarkable lack of consensus on the most appropriate design of local government expenditures and revenues across Canada, but as providing room for some out-of-the-box thinking on this question. Having said this, we are cognizant of the need to keep our feet on the ground. As such, we divide our recommendations into two sections: what we call some "modest proposals," that can be imposed by and largely within the framework of the current system with some "tinkering," and some "immodest" proposals that require more fundamental reform. Before beginning, it is useful to briefly describe some basic principles that have guided us in our thinking.

The defining characteristic of local government jurisdictions is that they are small, both economically and geographically. They are also "open" in the sense that labour and capital are relatively mobile across local jurisdictions. We suggested earlier that the general trend toward what has been referred to as "globalization" has likely increased the "openness" of local governments. Thus Toronto must now increasingly compete for capital and skilled workers not only with Calgary and Montreal but also with Chicago and New York. These characteristics of local jurisdictions mean that local governments should avoid tax and expenditure programs, the purpose of which is income redistribution. Such efforts will drive the more heavily taxed out of the local jurisdiction and attract those treated favourably.

Recognition of this has led public finance economists to stress the use of the benefit principle, as opposed to the ability-to-pay principle, when evaluating local government expenditure and tax choices. The benefit principle asserts that those who pay taxes or other types of charges to finance local government expenditures should also be those who benefit from those expenditures. The ability-to-pay principle asserts that those paying taxes or other types of charges required to finance local government expenditures should be those with the greatest ability to pay. The ability-to-pay principle thus emphasizes that the distribution of the tax burden should vary across different income (or ability to pay) groups, while the benefit principle emphasizes that the tax burden should fall on those who benefit from local government expenditure, regardless of their income.

The attraction of the ability-to-pay principle as a criterion for tax design varies inversely with the ability of the more heavily taxed to flee the government's jurisdiction. As one moves down the ladder from national to provincial to local governments, the ease with which the more heavily taxed can escape the jurisdiction increases and the ability of governments to engage in active income redistribution via an application of the ability-to-pay principle becomes more and more difficult. For this reason, public finance economists argue that the ability-to-pay principle should play a smaller role in the analysis of local public finance than the benefit principle, and that redistribution should fall primarily under the responsibility of provincial and federal governments.[8] In particular, city governments should resist the temptation to use local taxes and other fees as an income-distribution tool. Having said this, there are times when a strict application of the benefit principle is not possible, and there are times when, from an efficiency perspective, it is not desirable. As such, our application of the principle will be admittedly somewhat uneven. There are many things to balance.

The usefulness of the benefit principle as a criterion for tax design rests on the ability to identify the beneficiaries of government expenditures and the ability to charge these beneficiaries amounts that accurately reflect the true cost of providing these services. These considerations restrict the types of expenditure responsibilities and the types of revenue sources that should be assigned to local governments. Application of the benefit principle requires that local government expenditures be restricted to areas where the benefits can be clearly assigned and requires that local governments be assigned access to types of revenue that can accurately reflect the private benefit received. Thus local taxes and charges should as closely as possible mimic market prices. By doing so they encourage the efficient consumption of local government provided goods and services.

The assertion that the benefit principle is the appropriate criteria for allocating the burden of financing local government expenditures is often associated with Richard Musgrave (1983) and was recently restated by Wallace Oates (1996, pg. 36) as follows:

> Lower levels of government ... should, as much as possible, rely on benefit taxation of mobile economic units, including households and mobile factors of production. To the extent that non-benefit taxes need to be employed on mobile economic units, perhaps for redistributive purposes, this should be done at higher levels ... of government. To the extent that local governments make use of non-benefit taxes, they should employ them on tax bases that are relatively immobile across jurisdictions.

For the most part, this is a view that we share and the benefit principle will play an important role as a unifying principle in much of what is to follow. We will find it useful to refer back to Oates' passage several times in the ensuing discussion.

One potential criticism of the Musgrave-Oates approach to local public finance, and in particular of its emphasis on the benefit principle, is that it ignores a problem of tax design known as vertical and horizontal tax externalities. Vertical tax externalities result when different levels of government in a federation access the same tax base. In this situation the choice of a tax rate at one level of government can affect the choices at other levels of government by affecting the size of the tax base. A horizontal tax externality results when a change in the tax rate by one government affects the choice of tax rates by other governments at the same level due to the mobility of tax bases between jurisdictions. Horizontal tax externalities are often associated with tax competition between jurisdictions.

While the theoretical arguments are compelling, the practical importance of fiscal externalities for local public finance ultimately rests on empirical considerations. How important are fiscal externalities in practice? Our reading of the literature is that the evidence regarding the role that vertical and horizontal fiscal externalities play in the setting of tax policy is somewhat mixed. Besley and Rosen (1998), for example, investigate the presence of vertical fiscal externalities for tobacco and gasoline taxes in the United States. They find that U.S. states tend to increase taxes on these goods in response to increases in the federal tax rate. Goodspeed (2000), on the other hand, in a study of 13 OECD countries finds the opposite effect—local governments tend to reduce taxes in response to an increase in federal taxes. In both cases, the responses are quite modest. In terms of horizontal externalities, most of the empirical work has focused on the presence of tax competition. Again, the evidence is mixed. Devereux, Lockwood and Redoano (2002) find some evidence of tax competition between OECD countries. Stewart and Webb (2003), on the other hand, find no such evidence. There have been few empirical studies of tax competition at the local level.[9]

In light of the mixed empirical evidence on the importance of fiscal externalities, we take the following approach, which we think of as a sort of middle ground. As a matter of first order importance, we think that arguments related to fiscal externalities are trumped by considerations associated with the benefit principle. This said, we qualify, constrain if you will, some of our recommendations in light of considerations related to vertical and horizontal fiscal externalities.

On a related point, the presence of fiscal externalities is often used to justify the presence of vertical fiscal imbalances and transfers from higher to lower levels of government. The idea is that concentrating tax policy at the centre, and transferring revenues to lower levels of governments, can eliminate inefficiencies due to both vertical and horizontal externalities. In light of the mixed empirical evidence and the importance we attach to the benefit principle, we are unconvinced of the need for provincial governments to transfer more by way of grants to municipal coffers. We hasten to add that this is not because we think that cities currently have enough money to do what they want, or are supposed to do, nor that the current level of provincial government transfers is appropriate.

As the previous section indicated, there is a wide range in the share of local expenditures financed by provincial government transfers in Canada. To be frank, we do not feel that we are in a position to pass judgement on these questions in any sort of quantifiable way. Rather, our view is that if a city government feels that it requires more money to do what is expected of it by its citizens, then it should be in a position to get that money from the people who will be the primary beneficiaries of the resulting expenditures and to whom they are ultimately accountable to at the ballot box—the citizens and voters of the city.

We think that this later point is vital, and points to an important connection between the benefit principle and political accountability. There is a natural complimentarity between the idea that those who benefit from a service should pay for it and the idea that those who spend the money to provide the service should raise it. It is important that local governments and local citizens be aware of and incorporate hard budget constraints when making spending decisions.

Overreliance on vertical fiscal transfers from provincial, and federal, governments not only softens the local budget constraint but, as we saw in Section 2, transfers can be an unstable and unreliable source of revenue. From the perspective of accountability, it is important not to break what Albert Breton (1996) refers to as the "Wicksellian connection" between the spending and taxing side of the budget. To put the matter more bluntly, to the extent possible, the government that spends the money should be the government that is responsible for raising the money.

The usual interpretation of the Musgrave-Oates approach to local public finance as it relates to the benefit principle is that local governments should rely largely on user fees and property taxes to finance the provision of local goods and services. This is an interpretation that we think has a good deal of merit and we find it interesting, as reported in Section 2, that local governments in Canada have, when fiscally stressed, resorted to greater reliance on just these revenue sources. We think it is appropriate then, that property taxes and user fees should continue to be very important sources of local government revenue into the foreseeable future. However, we are also of the view that provincial governments should "remove the shackles" that currently restrain local governments from accessing a broader range of tax bases.

In our view, cities should be allowed to impose a wider, though not necessarily unlimited, range of taxes, augmenting the current reliance on property taxes and user fees with other sources of revenue. Moreover, we argue that some of the current sources of revenue, particularly those associated with taxes on businesses, do not stack up well according to the standard evaluative criteria, including the benefit principle. While not wishing to be overly dramatic, in our view the shackles that bind local governments in Canada, and in Alberta in particular, are reminiscent of third world local public finance. It makes local governments unresponsive and unaccountable to the citizenry and the electorate, and it forces local governments to rely over much on an inefficient set of taxes. Allowing cities to exercise a richer set of tax instruments would, we believe, go a long way towards redressing this.[10]

As suggested above, we think that there is room for some out-of-the-box thinking on this question. Having said this, we are aware of the constraint of practicality. As such, we divide our recommendations into two sections:

modest proposals and immodest proposals. A warning is also in order. We lack both the time and resources to offer much in the way of very specific, quantifiable recommendations. Rather our recommendations are, of necessity, quite general. This is very much an exploratory thought piece intended to identify some issues that should be addressed by that reliable old standby, further research.

Some Modest Proposals

As documented by Vander Ploeg (2000) in a recent Canada West Foundation study, compared to Canadian cities, U.S. cities have access to an extremely wide array of tax bases. U.S. cities impose taxes as far ranging as income taxes, general sales taxes and selective sales (or excise) taxes. Some of these taxes are imposed and administered directly by the cities themselves; others involve revenue-sharing with the state. While we are not of the view that the complete range of tax bases available to U.S. cities should necessarily be opened up to Canadian cities, we do think that at the very least a modest expansion in the ability of cities to raise own-source revenues would be desirable.

User Fees. The benefit principle leads naturally to a discussion of user fees. Charging fees for the provision of local goods and services is, in fact, an area where cities currently have a good deal of latitude and, as far as we can tell, there is no need for the provincial government to take off the shackles in this regard—they are already off. We do, however, think that some of the thinking about user fees at the local government level has been somewhat misguided.

As noted above, municipalities in Alberta currently rely on user fees to a greater extent than municipalities in any other province (see Table 2). In 2001, municipalities in Alberta collected an average of 34 per cent of own-source revenues from user fees. This compares to an average of 26 per cent across the country. Without much more detailed information on the specific source of those fees, it is difficult to pass judgement on whether cities should rely more or less on user fees. Having said this, our suspicion is that an increased reliance on user fees in the revenue mix would not only be desirable from the perspective of the benefit principle, but is probably inevitable from a more practical perspective. While we cannot be more precise than this in terms of the overall level of user fees, we can offer some guiding principles that should be followed in setting the configuration of user fees.

First, the benefit principle in general, and its application to user fees in particular, requires that we be able to identify the user or, more generally, the ultimate beneficiary of the service. For many locally provided services this is not difficult (i.e., water, sewage, garbage collection, etc.). In other cases the ultimate beneficiary of the service may not be quite so clear-cut. But even in those cases where there is a clear link between the good or service being provided and the identity of the user, we advocate a modification to the typical approach to determining user fees, a modification that departs somewhat from a strict application of the benefit principle.

The standard approach to user fees suggested by the benefit principle is that such fees are both equitable and efficient. The equity aspect is clear: It is fair that those who benefit from the provision of a good or service should pay for it. The efficiency aspect requires some elaboration. Fees should be set so as to induce individuals to consume the efficient amount of the good in question. This requires that per unit charges be based on some notion of marginal cost.[11] Since city-provided goods and services often involve significant fixed costs, average costs tend to be much higher than marginal costs. These fixed costs must be financed in some way. One approach often advocated is a two-part tariff—a variable charge to cover marginal costs and a fixed fee to help cover fixed costs. The basic idea is that if user fees are set appropriately, properly reflecting marginal and average costs of providing the good or service, the fees can mimic market prices and promote the efficient consumption of local government goods and services.

While we think that this view has a good deal of merit, we also think that it is too narrow. If user charges are viewed from a broader perspective, as one of several sources of revenue to the local government, a different approach is required. Viewing a user charge as part of the entire revenue generation system, and not simply as a cost recovery mechanism for a particular good or service, the objective is to establish a configuration of tax rates and user charges so as to raise a given amount of revenue in the most efficient (excess burden minimizing) way possible. In this case, the most efficient configuration of user charges ought to reflect the application of the so-called Ramsey Rule. While familiar to public finance theorists, the implications of the Ramsey Rule are not, as far as we can see, reflected in the discussion of local user charges in practice.

The Ramsey Rule requires that user fees, and other taxes, be set so as to lead to the same percentage reduction in the quantity demanded of all goods and services provided by the local government. This means that goods and services that are quite responsive to price changes (elastic) should face low user fees or tax rates while goods that are less responsive (inelastic) should face higher user fees. Viewing a user fee as one of several possible sources of revenue available to the local government thus loosens the link between the fee charged and the marginal or average cost of actually providing the good or service.

Applying this idea to user charges suggests that some user charges should be greater than the (marginal) cost of providing the good or service and some should be less, depending upon the configuration of elasticities. Thus, the costs of providing a particular good or service enters the overall costs of government that must be financed by a broad array of taxes and user charges, and not covered by a particular charge. While this is by no means a unique or profound insight (the essence of it can be found in any undergraduate public finance textbook), we think that it does involve a change in the way that cities typically view user fees—they should be viewed from the broader perspective of raising revenue in an efficient manner rather than from the narrower perspective of covering the costs (marginal or otherwise) of providing a particular good or service.

Property Taxes. As indicated in Table 2, property taxes currently account for 53 per cent of total local government revenues in Canada, and 65 per cent of own-source revenues. Municipalities in Alberta are at the low end of the scale, with figures of 43 per cent and 51 per cent respectively. Property taxes are, and will continue to be, attractive as a source of revenue for cities for two reasons. The first arises from the failure of the benefit principle as it is applied to certain locally provided services. User charges can be levied on services where the individual beneficiaries can be identified and where exclusion is possible.

For some local government services, neither of these characteristics hold. Police and fire protection and general city administration are examples. However, we can identify the group of agents who benefit from these services (property owners, the citizens and businesses that reside in the city). The benefit principle suggests that this group should be responsible for footing the bill. Property taxes are one way of doing this. In this respect property taxes can be considered a sort of generalized, or nonspecific, user charge. Referring again to the earlier cited passage from Oates (1996), property taxes also have the merit of being imposed on an immobile factor—real property—and are therefore an efficient way to raise revenue.

We certainly do not intend to get into the minutia of property-tax design. However, we do have some general comments. The first concerns the financing of infrastructure related to municipal growth—new roads and interchanges associated with new development. The primary, though not the only, beneficiaries of this infrastructure are the individuals who live in the new subdivisions and the businesses that set up shop there. The benefit principle suggests that these agents should be primarily, though not exclusively, responsible for paying for the associated infrastructure. There are several ways of doing this. One is to impose appropriate lot levies on developers, which will be passed on to future homeowners and businesses in the form of higher lot prices. This is indeed a practice that is followed in most Canadian cities, including Alberta. Without more study we cannot say whether or not these lot levies are set at the appropriate level; indeed, we can't even say what the appropriate level may be. However, our suspicion is that lot levies may currently be set such that more of the costs of new infrastructure is being borne by existing homeowners and businesses than might be justifiable under the benefit principle. As such, we think that an argument may be made for higher lot levies on new development.

A second, related issue concerns the use of differential property tax rates as an economic policy tool. Without entering the debate on the costs associated with "urban sprawl," one way to discourage sprawl and reduce the size of the so-called municipal "footprint" is to impose differential property taxes that reflect the costs, including social costs, of sprawl. This is an approach that is followed in some cities, but not, to our knowledge, in Alberta municipalities.

Our third, and final, issue under the heading of property taxes concerns the taxation of nonresidential (business) property, including the imposition of separate business taxes. Without at this point entering into a discussion of the form of local taxes on businesses—we will address this issue later when we introduce our immodest proposals—there is a long tradition of questioning the economic case for local taxes on businesses at all. Charles McLure (1983), among others, has strongly criticized local business taxes as distorting location decisions and introducing significant efficiency costs because of the high degree of mobility of business capital, particularly across local jurisdictions. Referring yet again to the passage from Oates (1996), mobile factors are not in general good candidates for nonbenefit local taxes.

Having said this, and here we blatantly bow to political expediency, it seems to be inevitable that local governments will always and everywhere try to impose taxes on businesses for the simple reason that businesses do not vote. We will argue below that business and nonresidential property taxes currently levied by cities are not the best way to do this. However, if nonresidential property and other taxes are to be levied on businesses, we think that the current system leaves a lot to be desired.

Indeed, we do not need to rely solely on political expediency to justify the taxation of businesses at the local level (in whatever form). Once again, we can appeal to the benefit principle. Businesses benefit from the provision of the goods and services provided by local governments. Of course, as discussed above, when specific public services benefit identifiable individuals and businesses, user charges should be imposed. However, just as residential property taxes can be justified as a generalized benefit tax on individuals for local services that provide generalized benefits, so too can local taxes levied on businesses in the form of business taxes or nonresidential property taxes (or whatever) be justified as a form of generalized benefit taxation for businesses. Just like residents, businesses should pay for the services provided to them by local governments.

An important question then becomes what share of the generalized benefits associated with local government expenditures accrues to business versus residents? The answer to this question is obviously key to the implementation of the benefit principle and the setting of appropriate tax rates on individuals versus businesses. While this is a difficult assessment to make—several essentially arbitrary assumptions must be made—there have been some attempts to do so. In the case of the United States, Oakland and Testa (1998) estimate that the business share of state and local government expenditure is 13 per cent. Closer to home, Kitchen and Slack (1993) estimate that the business share of the benefits of noneducational local government expenditures is about 40 per cent on average (20 per cent if education is taken in to account).

What are the implications of this for the taxation of businesses by local governments, through property taxation or otherwise? While it justifies some level of business taxation by municipalities, those taxes should be in line with the benefits received by businesses. Again, more detailed consideration is required, but there are reasons to suspect that the current level of business taxes levied by cities in Alberta is too high. First, a split mill rate approach is followed in Alberta cities whereby nonresidential property is in fact subject to a higher tax rate than residential property of equal value. Second, in addition to the nonresidential part of the general property tax, businesses are subject to special business taxes, typically levied on the annual rental value of business property. This means that businesses in Alberta are taxed at a higher rate than residences on property of equal value. Given that, as suggested above, businesses benefit to a lesser degree than residents from local government expenditures, the fact that businesses face higher tax rates is inconsistent with the benefit principle.[12] As pointed out by Thirsk (1982), this severs the link between taxes and benefits essential to sound local public finance. We return to a discussion of local businesses taxes below when we present our immodest proposals.

Excise Taxes. What we refer to here as excise taxes comes under the heading of Consumption and Other Taxes in Table 2. We distinguish between excise taxes imposed on particular goods and services and a general sales tax imposed on a much broader range of goods and services. We focus here on the former; the latter is discussed below as one of our immodest proposals. As can be seen from the table, these taxes currently account for a miniscule share of both the own-source and total revenue of localities in both Canada in general and Alberta in particular.

We think that there is increased scope for the application of excise taxes by local governments. Vehicles are the bane of city governments. As seen in Table 1, one of the most important expenditure categories for local governments is related to transportation infrastructure—roads, bridges and interchanges. Cars and problems that are associated with them dominate local politics. While the entire citizenry benefits from the transportation infrastructure in so much as it is facilitates private sector activity, some of this benefit is directly proportional to one's use of the roads. This suggests the use of user charges for roads to finance part of the costs of building and maintaining the transportation infrastructure. Note our emphasis on the word "part." Drivers are not the only beneficiaries of roads, and some sort of generalized benefit tax to finance roads is also justifiable.

Of course the most direct means of collecting user charges for roads is tolls. While we think that this is something that should be seriously considered for specific road projects, a general set of tolls would be a substantial deviation from current practice and could be costly to impose and administer. The next best thing is to impose taxes on activities that are closely related to road use, which in turn leads naturally to consideration of gasoline taxes. The idea that fuel taxes can act as a user charge for roads is, of course, not new. We think that it is an idea that has considerable merit.

Currently in Alberta, Edmonton and Calgary both receive 5 cents per litre of the 9 cents per litre provincial tax levied on gasoline with the revenues distributed on the basis of gasoline sales in each city. While the argument for imposing fuel taxes, as a de facto user charge for roads, is compelling, gasoline taxes have several other added benefits as a revenue source for cities. One is that they are more responsive to changes in population than other sources of local revenue such as property taxes. At the same time, fuel consumption is relatively unresponsive to price changes (inelastic), and is therefore a good candidate for taxation on efficiency grounds (not to mention environmental arguments). In a similar vein, as a relatively immobile tax base (it is costly to transport or purchase elsewhere) it is also a good candidate for a nonbenefit tax for cities, of the type described in the Oates (1996) quotation.

We think that the current tax-sharing arrangement between the province and the two major cities in Alberta is a step in the right direction in terms of removing the shackles, but it doesn't go far enough. In particular, our understanding is that there is some question regarding the permanence of the arrangement, as is evidenced by the recent attempt on the part of the provincial government to substantially lower the cities' share of the tax (the provincial government has subsequently backed off this threat). In our view the provincial government must make a strong commitment to maintaining the current arrangement. But this is still not enough. As indicated above, an excise tax on gasoline is attractive as a local tax instrument for several reasons. We see no compelling argument for why cities should not be able to impose their own additional taxes on fuel without having to appeal to the provincial government to share tax points.

The immobility of gasoline as a tax base reduces concerns related to horizontal competition in tax rates across communities. If this is a concern, the provincial government might set a maximum additional fuel tax that may be imposed by municipalities, but as a general statement our view is that if local governments are able to convince local citizens that additional taxes on fuel are required to finance local expenditures then why not?

It all comes back to cars. Another possible source of revenue that should be opened up to cities is a fixed annual levy on vehicle registration. The argument should now be familiar. It is an immobile tax base (well, from a certain point of view), would be imposed on a very inelastic tax base and it plays the role of yet another type of generalized benefit tax as the number of vehicles in the city is closely related to the demand for local government goods and services—everything from roads to police and emergency services.

Some Immodest Proposals

The set of proposals discussed above can, as far as we can tell, be implemented without a good deal of fuss, or at least not much more fuss that is typically associated with city-provincial wrangling. As a part of our general theme of removing the shackles, consideration should be given to two other possibilities which might be somewhat more contentious.

The two proposals are in fact related. The first is to impose a sales tax in the province with the proceeds going to municipalities. The second is to revamp the local taxation of businesses, eliminating business and nonresidential property taxes and replacing them with a business value-added tax (BVT). We will briefly consider each in turn.

Sales Tax. Sales taxes are relatively common in U.S. cities. In Canada, as far as we know, no cities are involved in the general sales-tax field. Alberta is the only province in the country that does not impose a general sales tax at the provincial level. Our first immodest proposal is that Alberta implement such a tax at the municipal level, with the following features.

All, or a substantial portion, of provincial transfers to the cities would be cut. The provincial government would then reduce its personal income tax rate by the appropriate amount so as to leave the province in roughly the same revenue position. A province-wide sales tax at a common rate would then be imposed, all of the proceeds of which would go to municipalities (perhaps with a deduction for administration costs incurred on the part of the province). There are two ways in which the proceeds could be distributed amongst the municipalities. One would be formula-based; some sort of capitation approach. The other would be to allocate the revenues on the basis of sales. The former would cut any direct link between the level of economic activity in a municipality and the amount of revenue received (except in so much as it is reflected in population), the latter would keep this link in tact. Our preferred approach would in fact be a combination of the two, whereby some portion of the revenues would be allocated on the basis of sales across municipalities, the remainder would be formula-based.

Total provincial transfers to municipalities in Alberta in 2000 amounted to a little under $780 million. Using numbers from McKenzie (2000), eliminating these transfers would allow the provincial government to lower the personal income tax rate from the current level of 10 per cent to about 8 per cent. Generating a similar amount of revenue in sales taxes to be allocated to municipalities as discussed above would require a sales tax of about 2 per cent.[13]

There are several reasons why we think this is an idea that deserves serious consideration. First, a recent set of studies by McKenzie (2000) and Dahlby (2000) examined the elimination (or reduction) of the provincial PIT in Alberta and its replacement with a sales tax. These studies concluded that there would be sizeable static efficiency gains as well as a significant positive effect on provincial growth associated with a change in the tax mix. Independent of any consideration of city finances, such a move would be economically beneficial for Alberta.

Linking the reduction of the PIT and the introduction of a sales tax to the reform of municipal finances makes it even more attractive, for several reasons. Allocating the revenues of the sales tax largely (though perhaps not exclusively) on the basis of local sales would allow the sales tax to act much like a generalized benefit tax. The best base for a generalized benefit tax is a broad measure of overall economic activity, for it is this economic activity that tends to generate demand for local government services. A broad-based consumption tax is an ideal candidate in this regard. At the same time, however, unlike personal income taxes and natural resource royalties, in per capita terms consumption is relatively stable. As such, it would provide local governments with a relatively stable source of revenue that is closely related to economic activity in their own jurisdictions.

This later point deserves emphasis. As discussed in Section 2 of the article, provincial transfers are the single most volatile source of local government finance. As discussed, there is a tendency for "senior" levels of government to download fiscal stress to "junior" levels of governments by cutting transfers. We saw this in Alberta's response to reductions in federal transfers, which the provincial government passed in part on to local governments. We have also seen it in Alberta as transfers to local governments are often reduced in reaction to low natural resource royalties. Replacing volatile transfers to cities with a source of revenue associated with consumption would go a long way toward introducing stability to local public finance.

Note well that our proposal involves a sales tax levied at the same rate across the province. While we are not entirely convinced that allowing municipalities to set their own sales tax rates would be a disaster, administrative economies of scale and potential fiscal externalities suggest that some degree of centralization is preferred. There may be some concerns about tax competition between neighbouring municipalities and fringe communities. Setting the sales tax rate at the provincial level alleviates these concerns. Moreover, this would be no worse and probably better than the current state of affairs, whereby the process under which provincial-local transfers are determined is opaque, to say the least. Having said all this, consideration might be given to allowing individual municipalities to impose tax points on top of the general provincial rate, perhaps subject to a cap set by the province (all of the additional revenues raised by these additional tax points would stay with the city).

A system such as we describe here, where intergovernmental transfers are eliminated, or scaled back, and replaced with proceeds from a general sales tax, is not unique to us. Australia recently introduced a GST on a national level with features very similar to the proposal described here. In the case of Australia, of course, the issue was of federal to state transfers, but the idea is essentially the same.

A Business Value-Added Tax. The replacement of current local taxes imposed on businesses, in the form of nonresidential property taxes and businesses taxes based on rental value, with a more sensible alternative is motivated by similar considerations, as well as some additional ones. As indicated in our discussion of property taxes, we think that the current system of local business taxes leaves a lot to be desired.

Economists are sometimes accused of agreeing on almost nothing. An important matter, on which most agree, however, is that there is little to be said in favour of taxing businesses. Taxes levied on one aspect of business activity, as is the case with local business taxes and nonresidential property taxes, are even more problematic. The costs associated with taxing business are sufficient to persuade most economists that there is little, if anything, to be said on efficiency grounds for taxes on business in general, and more particularly for taxes on business capital. On the contrary, there may be substantial economic gains from reducing and even eliminating most existing business taxes. Most of the economic costs of business taxes are larger the more mobile capital is, and since capital is decidedly more mobile as we move from the international, to the national, to the provincial, to the local level, the general case against the taxation of business capital is even stronger at the local level.

For example, Helliwell (1998) has suggested that national borders still seem to be relatively "high" in the sense that they impose significant costs on transnational transactions between countries with different currencies, different laws and a physical "filter" through which most trade and investment transactions still have to pass. The borders between provinces, however, are less "high" in this sense so that interprovincial flows of factors and products may well be affected by policy differences. Helliwell and McKitrick (1999), for example, show that interprovincial capital mobility is much higher than international mobility, with the correlation between savings and investment for individual provinces in Canada being statistically indistinguishable from zero.[14] Since capital mobility across provincial borders is high, capital tax competition and its efficiency implications may thus be considerably more important at the provincial level than the national level. If it is difficult and costly to tax capital at the provincial level, then it is orders of magnitude more so at the local level.

However, despite all of this, there is a good economic case for some local taxation of business on generalized benefit grounds. An overriding theme throughout our discussion is that to the extent that particular public activities result in identifiable cost-reducing benefits being received by particular firms, they can and should be charged for the costs incurred in providing such benefits. Whenever feasible, user charges should thus be applied to business firms, as to any other direct beneficiary.

In addition to services provided directly to specific identifiable private firms by the public sector, however, a significant fraction of general public expenditures, particularly at the local government level, directly benefit businesses. While, as discussed above, we think that the taxes currently levied on business actually constitute a higher share of the taxes than might be justified based on estimated benefit shares, the point is that an efficiency case can be made for levying some form of generalized benefit tax on business to cover such "unattributable" benefits to productive activities.[15]

Moreover, as also suggested previously, the political realities of governing in a democratic society are such that business taxes are going to be imposed no matter what economists may say. The important question then becomes not whether we should impose provincial taxes on business—we are going to do so in any event—but rather how we should impose such taxes. In a recent article, Bird and Mintz (2000) present a proposal that we think would move local business taxation in the right direction. Bird and McKenzie (2002) expand on this proposal. The proposal is that current local (and even provincial) taxes imposed on business capital—nonresidential property taxes and business taxes—be eliminated and replaced with a business value-added tax (BVT).

The arguments for local business taxes based on the benefit principle suggest that a broad-based measure of business activity is best, as it is overall business activity that gives rise to business demand for local government services (not income, rent, or the value of business property). A broad-based levy neutral to factor mix should be imposed, such as a tax on value-added.

Businesses add value by combining labour and capital with other purchased inputs. The value added by labour is the cost of labour (wages and salaries), while the value added by capital is the cost of capital (both debt and equity). A BVT base would consist of firm revenues, less purchases of current inputs except labour, less depreciation allowances and less royalties paid to the crown. As such, the BVT is imposed equally on the value added by both capital and labour. This differs from the existing approach to business taxation, which imposes a much higher burden on capital.

Compared to a conventional value-added tax (VAT) like the GST, a BVT has two important distinguishing features. First, it is a tax on income, not consumption: that is, it is imposed on profits as well as wages or, to put it another way, on investment as well as consumption. Second, as a tax on production, rather than consumption, it is imposed on an origin rather than a destination basis.[16]

The arguments for levying and administering the BVT at the provincial level are more compelling than those for imposing a sales tax at the provincial level. Our recommendation would be for municipalities to eliminate their own business and nonresidential property taxes altogether. After making an appropriate downward adjustment to reflect the level of benefits received by businesses vis-à-vis residents, a province-wide BVT could then be implemented at a common rate. While this may introduce some concerns regarding accountability, these would be alleviated somewhat if it was clear that the revenues go strictly to local governments. In this case accountability is trumped by concerns related to fiscal externalities.

CONCLUSION

In this article we have briefly reviewed the state of municipal finances in Canada. We began with a review of the "fiscal facts" as they relate to municipal revenues and spending. What jumped out from that review was the general lack of consensus amongst the practitioners of local public finance—those assigned the task of setting local tax rates and choosing where to spend scarce resources—regarding preferred levels of spending and taxation. Some common themes were identified, however. Those local governments placed under the most fiscal stress have responded by cutting spending in less key areas, and replacing taxes on more-mobile taxpayers with taxes on less-mobile taxpayers. Another common theme is that a key source of fiscal stress for municipal governments has been the fiscal choices of provincial governments. Faced with cuts to their own revenues caused by reductions in federal government transfers, provincial governments have passed these cuts on to their municipalities in the form of reduced transfers. What's more, provincial governments have added a few shackles by cutting mainly unconditional, as opposed to specific-purpose transfers to cities, and in so doing reduced the fiscal flexibility of municipalities.

We then turned to a discussion of some of the theoretical literature on local government finance. On the basis of that review and in light of our review of the stylized facts of municipal finances, we argued that local governments should be given more flexibility in their ability to levy taxes in order to finance their activities. If local governments are to become more important players in the Canadian federation, we believe it is important that some new thinking be offered on the question of how that level of government should be allowed to finance expenditures. In this connection we offer a series of modest proposals, which can, in our view, be accommodated quite easily within existing arrangements. We also offer a couple of immodest proposals that involve more substantive changes in fiscal arrangements. The overriding theme of all of the recommendations is that the provincial government should remove the shackles that currently restrict the revenue-raising choices available to Alberta cities.

Notes

Without encumbering them with responsibility for statements and claims made in this article, we thank Bev Dahlby and conference participants for helpful comments. Finally, we acknowledge the support of the Social Sciences and Humanities Research Council.

1. Local general government revenues and expenditures are from CANSIM matrices 7094–7100 and 8489–8491. Population data is from matrix 0001. Data on provincial all-items CPI are from matrices 9941–9950.
2. We are assuming that local governments pay similar rates of interest on their debts. Relative changes in debt charges thus mainly reflect changes in relative debt levels.
3. As Table 2 shows, almost all intergovernmental transfers received by local governments come from the province. Thus while our statement suggesting that provincial governments were solely responsible for cuts to transfers is not absolutely accurate, the small size of federal transfers makes the statement all but 100 per cent true.
4. In particular, federal transfers have switched away from the specific-purpose transfers of the Established Program Funding and Canada Assistance Plan to the general-purpose transfers of the Canada Health and Social Transfer.
5. Kneebone and Chung (2003) have shown that the elimination of federal deficits between 1993 and 1997 resulted mainly from spending cuts and due to the good fortune of lower interest rates and speedier economic growth. They have shown as well that roughly one-third of federal spending cuts introduced between 1993 and 1997 was due to cuts in transfers to the provinces and one-fifth was due to cuts in the generosity of employment insurance. Recognizing that cuts to

federally financed employment insurance often force former EI recipients onto provincially funded welfare rolls, they suggest that it is fair to say that between one-third and one-half of federal efforts at deficit reduction over that period was enjoyed at the expense of provincial budgets.

6. As noted earlier, local governments in Newfoundland, and to a lesser extent Quebec, are the exception.
7. Local governments in Ontario were also stressed by the demand from the province that they take on a growing responsibility for provision of social services. Local governments in Saskatchewan were included in the list of the fiscally most stressed because of their experience with transfer cuts and despite the low rate of population growth in that province. Nova Scotia was omitted from the list of the highly stressed. Although local governments in that province suffered large and frequent cuts to transfers, these were matched by reductions in responsibility for spending on social services. In fact, these amounts were of an almost equal amount.
8. In terms of local government expenditures, of which we have very little to say in this article, this suggests the withdrawal of local governments from the array of social programs that involve direct income redistribution. This does not, in our view, mean that local governments should withdraw completely from what might generally fall under the rubric of "social programs," but rather that they should withdraw from social programs that involve direct and explicit income distribution. We feel that there is some limited role for cities to play in the provision of social programs that affect what might be called the "local social fabric" of the city. Justification for this comes from the idea that local charity can be thought of a public good. This reasoning suggests that some social programs can be considered to be a local public good that benefit not only the recipients of those programs, but the citizens of the city as well. While this argues for some role of cities in the provision of social services, we think that this role should be quite limited, for the reasons mentioned above, and restricted for the most part to programs that do not involve direct and explicit income distribution.
9. Theoretically, the impact of federal tax rates on local tax rates is in fact ambiguous. Moreover, there is no consensus in the literature on the welfare implications of tax competition.
10. It bears mentioning that by proposing that the provincial government remove the shackles on cities we are not advocating a tax grab. Allowing cities to raise more and different kinds of own-source revenue opens up the possibility of reducing provincial transfers, which can in turn be used to finance reductions in provincial taxes. Indeed, one of our immodest proposals discussed below recommends precisely this.
11. Depending on the good or service, the measure of marginal cost may include some adjustment that recognizes that social marginal costs deviate from private marginal costs due to externalities.
12. The higher split mill rate imposed on businesses is sometimes justified by the deductibility of property taxes for corporate income tax purposes. While this is may be true, the fact that many businesses are nontaxable for CIT purposes and/or pay quite low income taxes by virtue of being subject to the small business tax rate, makes this a matter open to debate.
13. These numbers should be considered very rough. More detailed analysis is required to refine them.
14. As Dahlby (2000) shows, one must be cautious in interpreting correlations between saving and investment as reflecting capital mobility. In a simple endogenous growth model for a small, open economy, for example, a higher savings rate results in more investment in human capital and, since human

capital is complementary to physical capital, also in an increase in the investment rate.
15. Feehan (1998) argues that much government spending produces services that enhance the productive capacities of firms and provides an interesting theoretical rationale for such a tax under certain conditions. As Bird (1996) notes, this benefit argument for imposing "tax-prices" in the form of a generalized business benefit tax should not be confused with some of the less tenable versions of the benefit rationale for taxing corporations that may be found in the literature.
16. From one perspective, a system in which, in effect, two different types of value-added tax are imposed simultaneously might seem odd. But the apparent oddity resides largely in the similarity of the names. If it makes sense to levy taxes on both consumption and income in terms of base, as it may, it may equally make sense to levy one or both (or parts of each) indirectly in the value-added form at the business level as well as directly on income and/or consumption at the personal level.

References

Besley, T. and H. Rosen (1998), "Vertical Externalities in Tax Setting: Evidence from Gasoline and Cigarettes," *Journal of Public Economics* 70(3): 383–98.

Bird, R. (1999), "Rethinking Subnational Taxes—A New Look at Tax Assignment," IMF Working Paper, October.

Breton, A. (1996), *Competitive Governments: An Economic Theory of Politics and Public Finance* (New York: Cambridge University Press).

Courchene, T. (1997) *The Nation State in a Global/Information Era: Policy Challenges*, T. Couchene, ed., The Bell Canada Papers on Economic and Public Policy 5, John Deutsch Institute for the Study of Economic Policy (Kingston, Ont.: Queen's University).

Dahlby, B. (2000), "Tax Reform and Economic Growth in Alberta," Canada West Foundation Paper 200015.

Devereux, M., B. Lockwood and M. Redoano (2002), "Do Countries Compete over Corporate Tax Rates?," Centre for Economic Policy Research Discussion Paper DP3400, London.

Feehan, J. (1998), "Optimal Provision of Hicksian Public Inputs," *Canadian Journal of Economics*, 31, 693–707.

Goodspeed, T. (2000), "Tax Structure in a Federation," *Journal of Public Economics* 75, 493–506.

Kitchen, H. (2000), "Provinces and Municipalities, Universities, Schools and Hospital: Recent Trends and Funding Issues" in H. Lazar, ed., *Towards a New Mission Statement for Canadian Fiscal Federalism*, Institute for Intergovernmental Relations (Montreal: McGill-Queen's University).

——— and E. Slack (1993), "Business Property Taxation," Discussion Paper Series 93–24, Government and Competitiveness, School of Policy Studies, Queen's University: Kingston, Ont.

Kneebone, R. and J. Chung (2003), "Where Did the Debt Come From?," forthcoming in C. Ragan and W. Watson, eds., *Is the Debt War Over? Lessons from Canada's Battle Against Government Budget Deficits* (Montreal: Institute for Research on Public Policy).

——— and Melville L. McMillan (1985), "Local Government and Canadian Federalism," in vol. 63 of Studies for the Royal Commission on the Economic Union and Development Prospects for Canada, Richard Simeon, ed., *Intergovernmental Relations*, (Toronto: University of Toronto Press), 215–61.

Krugman (1991), "Increasing Returns and Economic Geography," *Journal of Political Economy*, 99(3).

McLure, C. (1983), "Assignment of Corporate Taxes in a Federal System," in *Tax Assignment in Federal Countries*, C. McLure, ed., Centre for Research on Federal Financial Relations (Canberra: Australian National University).

McMillan, Melville L. (forthcoming a), "Designing Local Governments for Performance," chap. 11 in vol. 5 of the Handbook on Public Sector Performance Reviews, Robin Boadway and Anwar Shah, eds., *Fiscal Federalism: Principles and Practices* (Oxford: Oxford University Press for the World Bank).

―――― (forthcoming b), "A Local Perspective on Fiscal Federalism," chap. 7 in vol. 6 of the Handbook on Public Sector Performance Reviews, Anwar Shah, ed., *Macrofederalism and Local Finances* (Oxford: Oxford University Press for the World Bank).

Musgrave, R. (1983), "Who Should Tax, Where and What?," in *Tax Assignment in Federal Countries*, C. McLure, ed., Centre for Research on Federal Financial Relations (Canberra: Australian National University).

Oakland, W. and W. Testa (1998), "Can the Benefits Principle be Applied to State-Local Taxation of Business?," Research Department Working Paper 98–16, Federal Reserve Bank of Chicago: Chicago, Ill.

Oates, W. (1996), "Taxation in a Federal System: The Tax Assignment Problem," *Public Economics Review* (Thailand) 1: 35–60.

Prime Minister's Caucus Task Force on Urban Issues (2002), Canada's Urban Strategy: A Blueprint for Action, Chair: Judy Sgro, November.

Stewart, K. and M. Webb (2003), "Capital Taxation, Globalization and International Tax Competition," University of Victoria Working Paper EWP0301, Victoria, Canada.

TD Bank Financial Group (2002), The Choice between Investing in Canada's Cities or Disinvesting in Canada's Future, TD Economics Special Report, www.td.com/economics, http://www.td.com/economics, April.

Vander Ploeg, C. (2002), *Big City Revenue Sources: A Canada-U.S. Comparison of Municipal Tax Tools and Revenue Levers* (Calgary: Canada West Foundation).

―――― (2002), *Framing a Fiscal Fix-Up: Options for Strengthening the Finances of Western Canada's Big Cities* (Calgary: Canada West Foundation, January).

Comments on "Removing the Shackles"

BEV DAHLBY

THE KNEEBONE AND MCKENZIE ARTICLE PROVIDES a useful survey of the trends in local government finances in Canada, and some interesting and provocative proposals for changing the way local government is financed. I will only provide a few brief comments on the "Stylized Facts" section and the authors' proposals for reforming the financing of the local government sector.

To begin, one general comment applies to both sections of the article. The title of this volume, and the subtitle of Kneebone and McKenzie's article, is "Paying for Cities," yet the statistics in the Stylized Facts section relate to the total local government sector, which includes large cities, small cities, towns and villages, and rural municipalities. Of course, Kneebone and McKenzie are limited by the available data from Statistics Canada, but most of the public attention, as these titles indicate, has been focused on the "fiscal plight" of Canada's large cities. Consequently, we are not yet in a position to evaluate the trends, and differences in experiences, of the large cities in different provinces. To address the question of the financing of cities, we need a more specific data set that relates only to the 10 to 15 large cities in Canada. The precise definition of a large city is, of course, highly subjective, and the appropriate working definition might vary from province to province.

The importance of distinguishing between large cities and other types of local government also arises in the discussion of the proposals for reforming local government finance. Some of the Kneebone and McKenzie proposals seem to address the concerns of the large cities, but would not be well suited for small centres and rural municipalities. Other proposals, such as their sales tax and business value-added tax proposals, would apply to all local governments in a province, but there would clearly be conflicts between the rural municipalities in Alberta and the cities of Edmonton and Calgary regarding the distribution of those revenues. I will return to that issue later.

One overriding impression from the statistical analysis provided by Kneebone and McKenzie is that the local government sector is quite small in the Atlantic region compared with the rest of the country. For example, as shown in Table 1, local government program spending as a percentage of total provincial-local program spending was 8.5 per cent in Newfoundland, 5.3 per cent in PEI, 11.8 per cent in New Brunswick and 16.6 per cent in Nova Scotia in 2000. (The relatively high figure for Nova Scotia, compared to say New Brunswick, is due to the $162 per capita spending on education by local government in Nova Scotia.) By contrast, local government's share was 27.5 per cent in Ontario, 15.4 per cent in Quebec and 15.9 per cent in BC. The high figure for Ontario is largely due to the $477 per capita spent by local governments on social services.

Why is local government in Atlantic Canada so small? Why is local government in Ontario so big? One possibility is that the provinces of Atlantic Canada are geographically "small," and therefore the provincial governments are "closer to the people" than they are in larger, and more diverse, provinces such as Ontario. Therefore the Atlantic provinces do need local governments to obtain the benefits from close contact between voters and politicians that local government provides in other provinces. PEI, due to the small size of both its population and area, is really just a glorified local government. So the issues regarding the role and financing of local government may be quite different in the larger provinces that they are in Atlantic Canada. Flexibility in defining the role of the local government sector would seem to be very desirable, and a good reason for retaining our current constitutional division of powers that makes the organization of the local government sector a provincial jurisdiction.

I will now make a few general comments about the Kneebone and McKenzie reform proposals. First, what problem are these proposals meant to solve? To my knowledge, no one has convincingly demonstrated that there is a vertical fiscal imbalance in the federation in the sense that the majority of Canadians would like to see more spent on the services provided by local governments (and large cities in particular) and less spent on the services provided by the federal and provincial governments. Some very informal polling of undergraduate students in my public finance classes indicates that there is no systematic underprovision of local government services. Yes, students would like to see more spent on streets, roads and urban transit, but they would also like to see cuts to fire protection, garbage collection, local parks and public libraries. Of course, not too much should be read into these polling results because the sample is small and not representative of the Canadian population as a whole. On the other hand, it suggests that there may be imbalances in funding different types of local government services, but no systematic underfunding of the local government sector. Those who claim that cities are in a "fiscal plight" need to provide clear evidence that city residents want across-the-board increases in the city services, and that they are prepared to give up services provided by the federal and provincial governments to pay for their expansion.

Kneebone and McKenzie acknowledge that there is no clear-cut evidence of "fiscal plight." Their proposals are meant to make provision of local government services more responsive to local needs. But would their proposals increase local accountability? I would argue that several of their proposals would not enhance accountability, and might even reduce local accountability, compared to the current system with its heavy reliance on property taxation. The reason is that gasoline tax (as currently constituted in Alberta), the sales tax and business value-added tax proposals are essentially revenue-sharing mechanisms. They would not increase the ability of cities to set tax rates in order to fund higher or lower levels of city services, and therefore local accountability would not be enhanced. Revenue sharing means that some forms of revenue, collected by the province, are dedicated to the local government sector. One advantage of this arrangement, as Kneebone and McKenzie point out, is that local government revenues would become less volatile, especially if the dedicated tax bases, such as the sales-tax base, are relatively stable. However, one government's volatility is another government's flexibility. If the provincial government cannot vary the revenues that it transfers to the local government sector, when it receives a fiscal shock (such as a cut in federal transfers) it will have to adjust by raising provincial taxes, cutting provincial services or running higher deficits. It is not clear that isolating the local government sector from the province-wide fiscal shocks would improve our fiscal performance. The experiences of other countries, such as Argentina where revenue sharing between the central and provincial governments has been blamed for the failure to engage in the necessary fiscal adjustments that precipitated the devaluation of the peso, suggest that we need to be very careful about adopting wide-ranging revenue-sharing arrangements between levels of government in Canada.

Another issue that arises with the Kneebone and McKenzie revenue-sharing proposals is the division of the revenues among local governments, especially the division between cities and rural areas. They recommend that a provincial sales tax might be distributed using a formula that would take into account both sales and population. It is clear that allocating the revenue on the basis of sales would favour the urban centres in Alberta, especially Calgary and Edmonton, because rural Albertans and residents of the smaller centres spend more money per capita in the large centres, buying items that are not readily available in their communities, than Calgarians and Edmontonians spend in rural areas. The per capita distribution would likely favour rural Albertans and residents of small communities because their per capita consumption expenditures are probably lower than in the urban areas. Given the political power of rural Alberta, one can confidently predict that any formula adopted by the provincial government would be heavily weighted toward a per capita distribution of sales tax revenues. Thus, the Kneebone and McKenzie sales-tax proposal might make the residents of Calgary and Edmonton worse off if the provincial government adopted their sales tax proposal and cut back on grants to municipalities. There would be similar problems with allocating the business value-added tax.

These problems with the allocation of the revenues from their "immodest" proposals do not mean that they should be dismissed out of hand, because we know that there are lots of problems with the property tax, especially the nonresidential property tax. What it means is that the distributional effects and the loss of accountability that would result from the adoption of their proposals need to be carefully weighed against the efficiency gains. Before such proposals are embraced, more detailed study is required.

Finally, Kneebone and McKenzie argue strongly for more emphasis on user charges to finance local government. Like many public finance economists, I strongly endorse their recommendation. However, most local governments would face major obstacles if they attempted to implement user fees, especially if Kneebone and McKenzie's suggestion, that the Ramsey Rule be adopted in setting user fees, is taken seriously. The information that is required for implementing or expanding user fees may be prohibitively costly for most local governments. The provincial government could help in this regard if it funded applied research that would help local governments analyze the allocative, distributional and administrative aspects of expanding the use of user fees.

ROBERT YOUNG — The Politics of Paying for Cities in Canada

INTRODUCTION

MOST POLITICAL SCIENTISTS KNOW LITTLE ABOUT politics. They spend their time reading or analyzing information, not observing and interacting with politicians, gaining their trust and learning their secrets. The polite way to make this point is to say that political scientists, like other observers, can never know exactly how a policy was made, and can only speculate about why it happened and why it took the form it did. This is referred to as the "black box" problem. The deep interior of the state, the micro-processes of policy formation, and the motives of state actors are not accessible to observers, who can only seek correlations of the forces observed to be weighing on decisionmakers with the policies that pop out of the state machinery.

The current raft of federal legislation about First Nations governance, for example, could be attributed to increasing Aboriginal poverty, decreasing band-council accountability, rising costs of the nonsettlement of land claims, declining sympathy with Aboriginal peoples' demands for autonomy or some combination of all of these and other factors. These antecedent changes can be documented and the legislation, as a function of them, explained. We can even trace how justificatory arguments by responsible politicians refer to these changes. But it will probably never be known whether or not Eddie Goldenberg breathlessly told Prime Minister Chrétien about some recent poll results, and it certainly will never be known whether Aline Chrétien ever leaned toward her husband and suggested, *"Tu dois faire quelque chose pour les autochtones, Jean, avant de partir."*[1]

At the moment, there is a ferment in the Canadian municipal world and in our thinking about it, and new initiatives are materializing, particularly from the federal government. The rising tide of urbanization is said to be creating new, irresistible demands. Globalization is making cities crucial for competitiveness and there are bound to be repercussions from the structural and institutional changes enacted in most provinces over the past several years (for they have been greater than anything witnessed since the 1960s). Political power is shifting to urban movements and cosmopolitans, and there are new ideas emerging into currency—smart growth, creative cities, social inclusion—that suggest new policy gaps and potential state initiatives. All this might be true. But it could also be true that the proximate cause of federal urban policy is that Toronto Liberals want revenge on the Harris Tories or that John Manley sees therein the best way to chip away at the Martinites.

Of course, there is a serious side to this. Political actors make all the decisions about all the policies that will shape the future of cities, and we ultimately cannot know why the policy happens. So the deepest politics of paying for cities in Canada is inaccessible to us. However, political actors are constrained and influenced by the broad forces that are bearing on them and that are observable. Long ago, when the study of public policy was just reemerging in the discipline of political science, Richard Simeon wrote that it is decisionmakers who "actually make the formal decisions and carry them out. It is *through them* that the broader political forces operate" (1976: 576, italics in original). What are these broader political forces? Roughly speaking, political scientists tend to invoke the economic and structural environment within which decisions are taken, the constraints and opportunities inherent in established institutions, the distribution of power in society and the sets of contending ideas that are in "good currency." Along with the actors involved and the micro-processes of decisionmaking, these factors explain policy outputs. They are used here as a framework to explore some aspects of the politics of paying for cities.

THE POLICYMAKING ENVIRONMENT

The big environmental pressure acting on the municipal question is, of course, globalization. This phenomenon often seems to be the ultimate cause of everything in contemporary social science. But as Mel Watkins recently commented, globalization is simply the current phase of capitalism (a nice line that quickly dissolves, like spun sugar). In reality, globalization is the aggregate of a set of changes—in transportation costs, trade patterns, migration, monetary flows and so on (Cable, 1995; Scholte, 2002). This is invoked as setting a context in which cities have become more prominent economic actors, with political and financial consequences:

> The reality of the new global order is that cities, especially those that fall into the category of global city-regions, have become major international players on the economic front. It is only natural that with this enhanced economic status, these city-regions will begin to strive toward some comparable recognition on the political front (Courchene, 2001: 282).

But even if the relative economic importance of major cities has grown, it is by no means inevitable that status and funding will follow. Institutions are sticky, and politicians make their own calculations when resources are scarce, as they always are.

A clearer impact of globalization—if rationales are taken as explanations—is the amalgamations in Montreal and Toronto (and perhaps Ottawa and Halifax). One common reason that was offered for these initiatives is the need for greater competitiveness. Empirically, this is inaccurate, as has been thoroughly argued by Sancton (1999; 2000). In amalgamations, costs tend to rise and efficiency to decrease, largely because wages adjust upwards, while in competitive U.S. cities such as Boston, the municipal structure is enormously fragmented. So the rationale does not hold; but it seems probable that these amalgamations have created monsters that will come back to haunt provincial governments with powerful demands on the fiscal front. Perhaps this is why the Campbell government in British Columbia seems content with the structure of Vancouver and the weak flexibility that characterizes the Greater Vancouver Regional District.

Another environmental element is the continuing fallout of September 11, 2001. Before the terrorist attacks, municipalities, provinces and Ottawa were cooperating with their U.S. counterparts in the creation of transportation corridors to facilitate NAFTA trade (Guillot, 2000). Now the "senior orders" of government are prepared to fund whatever is necessary to keep trade flowing as the U.S. border tightens. Curiously, there are few major cities right on the border, but in Windsor, Sarnia and Niagara Falls and further inland, where there are important air and rail nodes, large sums will be expended. The initial allocation under the Border Infrastructure Fund is $600 million, and if more is needed it will be found: this is imperative both politically and economically.

The final deep environmental factor is urbanization. Here the advocates of spending on cities invoke a mantra: Canada has become a highly urbanized country; over 80 per cent of Canadians live in cities; this trend will continue inexorably, and so on (Baillie, 2002: 3). But this is not the whole story, and certainly not the whole political story. First, much depends on definitions. The widely accepted "80 per cent urban" figure includes as "urban" anyone who does not live in a rural area. Hence, those living in villages of less than 2,500 people are urban. In fact, according to the fine detail available in the 1996 census, the sum of people living in towns of 5,000 or less combined with true rural dwellers makes up 30.3 per cent of the Canadian population. Those living in towns of fewer than 100,000 people made up 44.5 per cent of the population. The ten largest cities accounted for just 50.2 per cent of Canadians, while the so-called "C–5" cities (Toronto, Montreal, Vancouver, Calgary and Winnipeg) accounted for 37.8 per cent of the population (Statistics Canada, 1997: Tables 2 and 18).[2] Now, the population glass could be half empty or half full, but there obviously is a large proportion of the electorate that is not interested in paying for cities, especially very large ones. A resident of Chicoutimi-Jonquière (the twenty-first largest "city" in 1996) would seem to have no more inclination to support federal spending on the Gardiner Expressway or the Vancouver waterfront than would a lumberjack living in the bush in New Brunswick.

Moreover, the nonurban population possesses disproportionate voting power. Despite substantial reform in recent years, rural dwellers tend to be overrepresented in Canadian legislatures. First, at the federal level, the smaller, more rural provinces have lower electoral quotients than those that are more urbanized. In 2001, average population per seat was under 80,000 in Newfoundland (43.1 per cent rural), PEI (55.8 per cent), New Brunswick (51.2 per cent), and Saskatchewan (36.7 per cent), while Manitoba (28.2 per cent) was just over 80,000. The comparable electoral quotients in Ontario (16.7 per cent rural), BC (17.9 per cent), and Alberta (20.5 per cent) were over 100,000, while Quebec (21.6 per cent) was just under this (Courtney, 2001: Figure 11.6). So votes in the disproportionately rural provinces count for more. Second, there is malapportionment within provinces. In 1996 there were 56 House of Commons seats (18.8 per cent of the total) where the number of voters was plus or minus 10 per cent or more from parity (Courtney, 2001: calculated from Table 9.1). These seats are predominantly large urban seats or small rural ones. Again, rural dwellers are overrepresented.

Finally, there are the provincial governments, which are very interested in paying for cities—or not. Malapportionment is worse at the provincial level than the federal level (except in Ontario where the Fewer Politicians legislation made provincial ridings correspond with federal ones). Across all the provinces, 31.7 per cent of the legislative seats are more than plus or minus 10 per cent from parity (Courtney, 2001: calculated from Table 9.5). This is particularly acute in the deeply rural Maritimes provinces (52.2 per cent of the seats), but it is, more importantly, characteristic of three highly urbanized provinces—Alberta (39.8 per cent of the seats), British Columbia (38 per cent), and Quebec (52.8 per cent). So the power of the nonurban vote is further reinforced at the provincial level. Calculating the vote-weighted distribution of the Canadian population is beyond the scope of this article, but it would certainly push our 50.2 per cent living in the ten largest cities to well below 40 per cent at the federal level.

POWER

Largely for jurisdictional reasons, as will be elaborated in the next section, most of the power in the municipal-provincial-federal nexus lies with provincial governments. Of this raw fact, the municipalities and their supporters are keenly aware. To quote Albert Breton (2002: 15), who is among those now advocating substantial decentralization of jurisdiction and resources to the municipal order of government, the condition of local disempowerment is

> revealed by the incessant turmoil resulting from the decisions and actions of provincial governments delegating powers and responsibilities, sometimes with the financial means to implement the policies to which they give rise, sometimes not; reclaiming powers and responsibilities more or less without explanation; disallowing *bona fide* decisions of local governments; redrawing territorial boundaries of local jurisdictions; changing the rules of representation; deciding when and for what purpose local governments can and cannot borrow; defining and redefining tax bases; capping local tax rates; deciding who will and who will not be taxed locally; and so on and so forth—a veritable bedlam.

There is no doubt that such provincial actions, especially amalgamation, have recently made the politics of cities and of paying for cities much more visible and contentious. But the cities, at least as represented by the Federation of Canadian Municipalities (FCM), do not seem to be demanding more decentralization and new powers. They seek stability, and they seek more money. Only modestly do they hint at the rising public demand for their services (FCM, 2001: 11):

> The main concern of municipal governments is their capacity to finance, predictably and responsibly, the increasing functions and responsibilities they are being given, either by statute or public expectation. Municipal governments must change the way they finance their operations so that they can meet their growing responsibilities, ensure accountability, and develop their capacity to play an even more positive, productive and responsive role in Canada's political system.

This is the majority view, or perhaps the lowest common denominator among municipalities: they simply need more autonomous fiscal power. Among the bigger cities, however, there is the sense that power is shifting toward them.

The exception here is Toronto. This city has been hurt. Much of the impetus behind the rise of urban issues on the national policy agenda comes from a revolt of citizens living in downtown Toronto against their amalgamation with the suburbs and, further, against the entire "common sense revolution" of the Harris Tories.[3] Recall that the federal Liberals won 101

Ontario seats in 1997 with 49.5 per cent of the vote, and 100 seats in 2000 with 51.5 per cent of the vote. They own Ontario. It is true that the caucus and the Cabinet hold representatives from the 905 area code and other bastions of support for Mike Harris. But it is downtown Toronto that contains the Cabinet heavyweights: Allan Rock (Etobicoke-Centre), Bill Graham (Rosedale), David Collenette (Don Valley East) and Art Eggleton (former heavyweight, York Centre), as well as influential backbenchers such as John Godfrey (Don Valley West), Joe Volpe (Eglinton-Lawrence) and Judy Sgro (York West).

It was the last of these, a former councillor, who was chosen to lead the Liberal Party's Caucus Task Force on Urban Issues, which delivered its final report in November 2002.[4] A caucus task force was an entirely new device. It was clearly a response by the Liberal leadership to backbench pressure for action about urban matters and especially the plight of Toronto. Just as obviously, though, it provided the federal government with an excuse to do nothing on the urban file for the 18 months of the task force's mandate.

Some power flows from money. In the current fiscal structure of Canadian federalism, Ottawa's position is paramount. While the provincial governments' share of total government spending has risen steadily in post-WWII Canada, Ottawa's transfers to the provinces declined as a percentage of provincial revenues from the early 1960s through to 1995 (Bird and Chen, 1998: Figure 5). Similarly, provincial government transfers to municipalities dropped from 22.5 per cent of provincial expenditure in 1975 to 16.5 per cent in 1995, with transfers falling from 51.2 per cent of municipal revenues to 43 per cent (Bird and Chen, 1998: Table 2). As Siegel writes, municipal governments have long sought more autonomy, and freedom from conditional grants in particular; however, having partially achieved this during the 1990s, "at least some local governments wish that they had not been so successful in liberating themselves from provincial funding assistance" (2002: 36).

Since the late 1990s, the trend has changed for the senior orders of governments, but not for municipalities. Between the 1998 fiscal year and 2001, federal revenues rose 12.3 per cent. Despite a growth of 14.5 per cent in transfers to the provincial governments, surpluses were large. Total provincial revenues increased by 13.7 per cent. And what of the municipal governments? Their total revenues were up just 6.2 per cent, and total transfers to them were down by 10 per cent. Of those transfers, the federal government accounted for just 2.5 per cent (Statistics Canada, 2002).

But the federal government is obviously not prepared to mount a full-scale assault on urban problems. The original mandate of the caucus task force was circumscribed. The commitment about cities in the 2002 Speech from the Throne was similarly limited. One reason is money, of course.

Cities have the potential to be vast sinkholes for federal expenditures (and not just cities, for heavy urban expenditures would have to be extended to small communities, as in the infrastructure program). The FCM has endorsed an Association of Consulting Engineers estimate that the "municipal infrastructure deficit" amounted to $44 billion in 1996 (FCM, 2001: 14). It is perhaps $60 billion by now. Facing this cavernous pit, Ottawa has a large incentive not to create expectations of largesse that will not and cannot be fulfilled.

Another reason for federal restraint is jurisdiction (see below). But a final one is ideological. Politically, "Ottawa"—the federal Liberal Party—is pitted against the sovereigntist government in Quebec and right-wing governments in Alberta, BC and especially Ontario. The Mike Harris government cut provincial taxes sharply, on both individuals and businesses (Courchene with Telmer, 1998: 169–92). At the same time the government decreased expenditures and transferred responsibility to municipalities for many programs that had been provincially funded or cost-shared (in exchange for removing much of education funding from the property-tax base). So massive reductions in provincial service delivery (see Krajnc, 2000, for example) and the serious strain on municipal finances led directly to pleas for federal aid (to an Ontario contingent that is a majority in caucus). But, strategically, why would or should the federal Liberals spend to finance the common sense revolution? Why should Ottawa fill the service gaps left by Mike Harris? Federal-provincial partisan differences have led to restraint in bailing out municipalities and easing the pain caused by the Ontario Tories and by other cost-cutting and offloading provincial administrations.

INSTITUTIONS

Provinces have jurisdiction over municipalities under the Constitution Acts. Despite various enactments to recognize a superior status for local governments, such as Alberta's legislation extending "natural-person" powers to them, and the negotiation of a few special agreements with big cities and municipal associations, the provincial governments have sovereign power over cities. This is not going to change. As Bird and Chen put it: "The province proposes, and, on the whole, the province disposes" (1998: 61).

The provincial governments tend to guard their jurisdictional field, and the current federal government has been respectful of this. As already suggested, the caucus task force provided an outlet for energy and indignation, and an excuse for two years of inaction.[5] It was also given a narrow mandate. First, it was to consult with "citizens, experts and other orders of government," and the aim was to work "more collaboratively, *within our federal jurisdiction*, to strengthen quality of life in our large urban centres"

(Prime Minister's Office, 2001: 1, italics added). The list of topics upon which the group was to place special emphasis bore a close correlation with areas of federal jurisdiction.[6] In its interim report, the task force touched on these areas. It also recommended an integrated urban strategy, but the high priority initiatives were limited to national programs for affordable housing, infrastructure and transportation (Prime Minister's Caucus Task Force, 2002a). The final report kept to the same three items. It did recommend the appointment of a "designated minister" for urban regions, but this person would have no functional responsibilities for implementing any programs.

Finally, the committee was mindful of provincial responsibilities: "Provincial and municipal leaders need to be involved in decisions that affect them, particularly in those areas of policy that have an impact on budgets. Urban projects and programs should be designed to meet federal objectives, on the basis of plans and targets developed in partnership with provinces and municipalities" (Prime Minister's Caucus Task Force, 2002b: 6).

This approach is consistent with the Chrétien government's stance toward the provinces. It is true that federal politicians have been, and are, involved in deep disputes with some provinces—social policy with Ontario, Aboriginal policy with British Columbia, the Kyoto agreement with Alberta. It is also true that federal politicians and public servants can be manipulative and disdainful toward their provincial counterparts.[7] It is also the case that the federal government continues to insist that spending power is quite unfettered, and it has wielded it over provincial objections, most notably in the Millennium Scholarships initiative. But the larger pattern is not one of a centralizing federal government. Instead, recent years have witnessed the major delegations of power and money in the wake of the 1995 Quebec referendum (especially in manpower training), and the negotiation of the Canada-Wide Accord on Environmental Harmonization and of the Social Union Framework Agreement.

When there were intense pressures upon Ottawa to move fast on urban issues, but great suspicion in provincial capitals, the minister of intergovernmental affairs was insistent that "all three orders of government must work together, *mindful of their respective jurisdictions*" (Dion, 2001: 4, emphasis added). And the Prime Minister has also cleaved to this position. For example, Chrétien promised in September 2002 that Canadians "will see significant additional action, within our own jurisdiction, to build an urban infrastructure that makes our cities a magnet for talent and investment" (*Globe and Mail*, 21 September 2002).

But on the municipal front, like others, the respect for the institution of federalism is most acute in Quebec. Here, the province jealously guards its jurisdiction, while Ottawa is profoundly ambivalent, aiming for initiatives that will win support and expand the Liberals' strength in the province, yet mindful not to provoke nationalist counterattacks. Both the sovereigntists and the federalists have a big stake in Montreal, and this has resulted in a curious new creature—Montréal International. This is a vast partnership to promote the economic development of La Métropole. It has a 25-member board of directors headed by the former federal Liberal cabinet minister, Francis Fox. Members include the deputy minister of the provincial Department of Municipal Affairs and the Metropole, the deputy minister of the federal Economic Development Agency of Canada for Quebec Regions[8] and various municipal politicians and business leaders (including Jean Pelletier, head of Via Rail and former chief of staff to Chrétien). Partners include municipalities in the greater Montreal region and a number of economic organizations (including Quebec's Société générale de financement and the business association Manufacturiers et exportateurs du Québec). Specifically mentioned as well are seven federal ministries and seven provincial ones.[9] The organization has several functions: informing firms and potential immigrants about the city of Montreal, promoting coherence within several key sectors—aerospace, information technologies, life sciences and telecommunications—and increasing investment.

This is an unusually broad partnership with the capacity, in theory at least, to coordinate major private-sector initiatives with the programs and support available from both the federal and the provincial government. It represents something of a truce between the sovereigntist Parti Québécois government and the federalists in Ottawa. More precisely, it represents something of a bet between the two sides, with Chrétien predicting that economic growth will show the advantages of remaining in Canada, while the Premier at the time of the establishment of Montréal International, Lucien Bouchard, argued that sovereignty had to be built on the foundation of a strong economy (Young, 1999: 90). In any case, Montréal International and associated initiatives remind us that the politics of paying for cities in Quebec is unique in Canada.

A final point about institutions is that it matters how provinces exercise their oversight of municipalities and more precisely of municipal-federal relations. Political scientists have not investigated this matter systematically, but we know from studies of federal-provincial relations how important is the locus of interaction (Cairns, 1979). Provincial oversight can be seen as consisting of two components—intensity and agency. Intensity refers to the level of surveillance and control exercised over the relations between Ottawa and municipalities. It can range from demanding information to exercising veto power. Agency refers to the location of oversight, which can range from a line department to the ministry of municipal affairs or its equivalent, to central agencies like Finance, to the Premier's Office.

One would expect intensity and agency to be correlated and to vary with the nature of the policy. There should be more stringent oversight when the policy is visible, involves regulation rather than spending, is not in exclusive federal jurisdiction and necessarily entails provincial action. Intensity should also vary with the nature of the province, being weaker when the provincial and federal governments are ideologically congruent, the province is poor, small municipalities are involved and the provincial association of municipalities is strong. All this seems probable. It is part of the institutional framework that affects paying for cities (and also paying for things to happen in cities), but it is almost entirely unexplored.

IDEAS

Currently, there is a ferment of ideas around municipal matters. This condition arises, no doubt, from the abuse some cities have suffered and from consistent underfunding. The debates are testimony to the vitality of think tanks, especially the Canada West Foundation (the "Western Cities Project Discussion Papers") and the Canadian Policy Research Networks (the set of studies that emerged under the direction of Jane Jenson and Leslie Seidle). It also speaks, at one remove, to the influence of business leaders such as Alan Broadbent and Charles Baillie.

It also is flowing both from municipal leaders like Glen Murray and David Bronconnier and from the federal government, through its support for the Metropolis project and the Policy Research Initiative, many of whose themes—human development, social cohesion—cut into big-city issues. Strikingly absent from this ferment of ideas are the provincial governments, which have grudgingly granted some concessions to municipalities but have taken no new and creative role.

This may be because the municipalities themselves are not united on their goals. There seem to be three basic options. The first is to seek increased financing and more autonomy, in the sense that provincial governments will abjure from inflicting further shocks in the form of amalgamations or service offloading (what the Americans call "unfunded mandates"—requiring new programs without transferring the requisite funds to run them). Those adopting this position are essentially passive. They accept the traditional role of local governments as suppliers of hard services financed through local property taxation. And here there is a crucial distinction—between spending *through* cities and spending *in* them.[10]

The provincial and federal governments spend billions and billions of dollars in cities, delivering their own programs. In fact, almost every dollar spent by a senior order of government is spent *within* space administered in part by municipal authorities. But these monies are separate from the transfers made to municipalities to deliver their own services, or to cooperate in some program desired by the senior government. In this first, minimalist, local-government position, this is all perfectly fine. Spending by senior governments within the municipal boundaries will increase the tax base and thereby trickle down to the local government. In the meantime, these local authorities want fewer disturbances and more money to deliver the services for which they are responsible.

A second position is to demand more participation in joint policymaking. Part of the rationale here is to avoid unanticipated shocks. More important is the sense that many of the new problems, especially in big cities, are "horizontal" problems that cut across traditional areas of government jurisdiction and departmental responsibility. Hence, they cannot be dealt with through the traditional specialized and isolated agencies (which are dismissed as "silos"). Examples of the new problems include the integration of immigrants, crime, homelessness, innovation and sustainable growth.

In this view, the functional responsibilities of two or three orders of government must be coordinated so as to mount effective attacks on complex problems. This is a vision of contemporary issues that was strongly promoted by the Policy Research Secretariat and supported by the current federal clerk of the Privy Council, Alex Himelfarb. It also informs the research emanating from the Canadian Policy Research Networks (Bradford, 2002; Jenson and Mahon, 2002). It also helps define the current FCM position on a possible new minister—lukewarm, because of the risk of having urban matters become ghettoized in yet another policy "silo" (*Globe and Mail*, 19, 20 November 2002). So, in this second position, the municipalities are meant to be at the policy table, hopefully armed with higher and more certain funding, and with a bolstered status, but no new powers.

The third position is that the municipal order of government take on new powers and functions at the expense of the orders of others, primarily the provinces. This idea has not been thoroughly developed nor has it been baldly enunciated, but Tom Courchene's analysis of Ontario as a "North American region-state" can lead quickly to defining that state as essentially the Greater Toronto Area (GTA), and to suggesting that more powers must be allocated to it: "The more Toronto and the GTA embrace the concept of themselves as dynamic economic motors having to go head-to-head with competing North American global city-regions, the more likely that Queen's Park will be pressured to accommodate this via a greater degree of self-determination" (2001: 283–84). Courchene's prescription is for more formal relations with the other orders of government, more fiscal autonomy and more power "over a large range of policy areas, driven by the principle of subsidiarity," with some new powers being concurrent and some exclusive (282).

This is a radical position. Despite being inspired by the Toronto city-region, that jurisdiction has not argued seriously for more extensive powers. Except for more scope to enter public-private partnerships and, ominously from the provincial viewpoint, to offer tax incentives and loan guarantees to business, the Toronto demands currently fall into the second position: more revenue, more revenue sources and participation in policy formation where the city is affected (City of Toronto, 2000). The barriers to contemplating cities as a third order of Canadian government with greatly increased powers are very substantial. Many municipal politicians would be content with more funding, more money spent in their localities and fewer disturbances. The view upon which there appears to be convergence is the second one: cities should be consulted more and play a larger role in policymaking, preferably with extra resources. But of course, what pops out of the policy machine also depends on individuals, two of whom deserve some brief consideration.

ACTORS

Jack Layton won the leadership of the New Democratic Party (NDP) in January 2003. For 20 years he was on the Toronto City Council, and he recently served as president of the FCM. Layton's campaign platform had many planks but a major one was "building solutions for communities," and he is quite aware of how urban issues could favour the left (Layton, 2002). He advocates allocating three cents per litre from the federal gas tax to public transit, spending $1.7 billion per year on municipal infrastructure, remitting to municipalities 100 per cent of their GST payments ($450 million more per year) and spending $1.6 billion per year on affordable housing, with Ottawa contributing $616 million of this.[11]

The NDP leadership campaign did not attract enough media coverage to focus public attention on these or any other planks, but this could change. Although inexperienced in national politics, Jack Layton is a compelling speaker, and a politician with deep reserves of raw energy. He could open up a pathway into federal politics for urban activists and members of social movements and, perhaps, younger Canadians.[12] This new NDP focus certainly would help keep the issues of Canadian "communities" high on the national agenda. The other, more significant actor is of course Paul Martin. Martin has signalled in the past that he would be willing to contemplate a "new deal" for cities. This could involve allocating to municipalities some federal tax room.

As with the Kyoto accord, Martin has been careful to insist that new initiatives should only follow extensive consultations with the provincial governments (*Globe and Mail*, 13 July 2002). Martin is expected, sometime soon, to stake out his position on urban issues. He may do this—despite the probable divisions it would cause, the lack of any necessity for him to lay out a platform and the general irrationality of building a super-optimal coalition. If he does, the politics of paying for cities in Canada will become both more intense and more complicated.

CONCLUSION

This article has touched upon only a few aspects of the politics of paying for cities. The emphasis has been on the federal government, for this is where much attention has come to be focused, unusually for Canada. One conclusion that seems evident is that no great new initiatives are likely. The municipalities are not demanding revolutionary change; there is opposition from nonurban residents and from those many competing interests also seeking funding, and the provinces are not supportive of big new policy changes.

Arguably, the current system is pretty efficient, politically. The municipalities are restricted primarily to the property-tax base, which imposes tight spending constraints. Various infrastructure programs requiring them (and the provinces) to match federal funds similarly ensure that new projects are genuinely desired and politically defensible by representatives of all three levels of government.

What would improve matters are provincial guarantees that unfunded mandates would not be imposed on municipalities (though future provincial legislation could always reverse this). There might also be some access to the gasoline tax for public transit and municipal roads. This should probably come from the provincial governments, for transportation externalities are province-wide at best, and it might well consist of a share of provincial gas-tax revenues allocated on a per-capita basis. Finally, some observers have noted that municipal governments probably underborrow (Bird and Chen, 1998: 60–61). While cautionary arguments can be made against debt financing even of productive assets, it would be politically feasible for Ottawa to provide some tax relief on the interest earned on municipal bonds. This would allow local governments access to new sources of revenue, while continuing to make them responsible for funding their own initiatives.

So the prospect is for incremental adjustments in policy about Canadian cities. Nevertheless, with shifts in the distribution of political power, more new ideas and especially the emergence of new political actors, the politics of paying for cities could radically change.

Notes

1. "You have to do something for the Native people, Jean, before you leave."
2. There is also the problem of nonurban people within census metropolitan areas (CMA). The Halifax CMA, for example, is the thirteenth largest in Canada, with 320,501 people in 1996. However, it covers over 2,500 square kilometres, and includes over 60,000 persons classified as rural; in fact, rural dwellers made up 19.5 per cent of the population. Similarly, the Montreal CMA includes such "urban" places as Hudson, Saint-Canut and the fringes of Varennes and Saint-Jérôme (Statistics Canada, 1997, Tables 8, 18 and 7).
3. The ire continues: see Barber, 2002.

4. Formally, this was the Prime Minister's Caucus Task Force on Urban Issues.
5. It was established in May 2001 and was, from the outset, to report by December 2002. Any subsequent initiative would take a few months to prepare, at least.
6. These were economic competitiveness, environmental issues, cultural assets, urban transit, settlement and integration of immigrants ("bearing in mind existing agreements with provinces"), at-risk populations—Aboriginal people, immigrants, disabled people and the homeless—and crime-related issues.
7. A remarkable example was provided by David Anderson's comment about the Kyoto disagreements. "Provinces will be provinces," he said. "They're all doing what every province is expected to do and ... [to] huff and puff and make sure my province pays less and therefore other provinces pay more" (*Globe and Mail*, 19 October 2002).
8. This, according to its website, is "better known as Canada Economic Development, the Agency or just CED." It has 14 offices across Quebec. (http://www.dec-ced.gc.ca/asp/General/Main.asp?LANG=EN, accessed on 23.11.02).
9. Visit http://www.montrealinternational.com/fr/profil/partenaires.aspx (accessed on 23.11.02).
10. I am grateful to my colleague Andrew Sancton for continuing to insist on this distinction, though he may not agree with the uses to which I put it.
11. See http://www.jacklayton.ca/jacks_vision/default.asp?load=communities (accessed on 24.11.02).
12. Early in the campaign, Layton enlisted the support of Steve Page, the leader of the popular band Barenaked Ladies. Tickets to the concert were free with the purchase of a $25 NDP membership (*London Free Press*, 13 September 2002).

References

Baillie, Charles (2002), "Brave New Canada," speech to the Canadian Club, Ottawa, Ontario, 19 March.

Barber, John (2002), "Pass the cap for core taxpayers," *Globe and Mail*, 21 November.

Bird, Richard M. and Duan-jie Chen (1998), "Federal finance and fiscal federalism: The two worlds of Canadian public finance," *Canadian Public Administration*, 41: 51–74.

Bradford, Neil (2002), "Why Cities Matter: Policy Research Perspectives for Canada," Discussion Paper No. F/23, Canadian Policy Research Networks (Ottawa: CPRN).

Breton, Albert (2002), "Federalization (Not Decentralization) as an Empowerment Device," presented to the C.D. Howe Institute Policy Conference on "Who Decides? Democracy, Federalism, and Citizen Empowerment," Toronto, 14–15 November.

Cable, Vincent (1995), "The Diminished Nation-State: A Study in the Loss of Economic Power," *Daedalus*, 124: 23–53.

Cairns, Alan C. (1979), "The Other Crisis of Canadian Federalism," *Canadian Public Administration*, 22: 175–95.

City of Toronto, Staff Report (2000), "Towards a New Relationship with Ontario and Canada" (Toronto: n.p.).

Courchene, Thomas J. (2001), *A State of Minds: Toward a Human Capital Future for Canadians* (Montreal: Institute for Research on Public Policy).

Courchene, Thomas J. with Colin R. Telmer (1998), *From Heartland to North American Region State: The Social, Fiscal and Federal Evolution of Ontario* (Toronto: University of Toronto).

Courtney, John C. (2001), *Commissioned Ridings: Designing Canada's Electoral Districts* (Montreal: McGill-Queen's University Press).

Dion, Stéphane (2001), "Municipalities and the Federal Government," notes for an address by the Honourable Stéphane Dion, President of the Privy Council and Minister of Intergovernmental Affairs, Annual General Meeting, Federation of Canadian Municipalities, Banff, Alberta, May 26.

Federation of Canadian Municipalities (2001), *Early Warning: Will Canadian Cities Compete? A Comparative Overview of Municipal Government in Canada, the United States and Europe*, prepared for the National Round Table on the Environment and the Economy (Ottawa: FCM).

Guillot, Romain (2000), "The Settlement of Land Transportation Trade Corridors Between the United States and Canada in Ontario Since the NAFTA," BA Honours thesis, Department of Political Science, University of Western Ontario.

Jenson, Jane and Rianne Mahon (2002), "Bringing Cities to the Table: Child Care and Intergovernmental Relations," Discussion Paper No. F/26, Canadian Policy Research Networks (Ottawa: CPRN).

Krajnc, Anita (2000), "Wither Ontario's Environment? Neo-Conservatism and the Decline of the Environment Ministry," *Canadian Public Policy*, 26: 111–27.

Layton, Jack (2002), "To the barricades: Battle for the community agenda," *Globe and Mail*, 2 September.

Prime Minister's Caucus Task Force on Urban Issues (2002a), "Canada's Urban Strategy: A Vision for the 21st Century," interim report (Ottawa: n.p.).

——— (2002b), "Canada's Urban Strategy: A Blueprint for Action," final report (Ottawa: n.p.).

Prime Minister's Office (2001), "Prime Minister's Caucus Task Force on Urban Issues Announced," press release, 9 May.

Sancton, Andrew (1999), "Globalization does not require amalgamation," *Policy Options* 20, November: 54–58.

——— (2000), *Merger Mania: The Assault on Local Government* (Montreal: McGill-Queen's University Press for the City of Westmount).

Scholte, Jan Arte (2002), "Globalization and the Rise of Supra-Territoriality," presented to the International Political Science Association conference on "Gérer la mondialisation," Montreal, October 24–26.

Siegel, David (2002), "Urban Finance at the Turn of the Century: Be Careful What You Wish For," in Edmund P. Fowler and David Siegel, eds., *Urban Policy Issues: Canadian Perspectives*, 2nd ed. (Don Mills: Oxford University Press), 36–53.

Simeon, Richard (1976), "Studying Public Policy," *Canadian Journal of Political Science*, 9: 548–80.

Statistics Canada (1997), 1996 Census of Canada, *A National Overview: Population and Dwelling Counts*, Cat. No. 93–357–XPB.

——— (2002), Local general government revenue and expenditure, Canada; provincial and territorial general government revenues and expenditures, Canada: at http://www.statcan.ca/english/Pgdb/govt06a.htm and /govto4.htm (accessed on 22 November 2002).

Young, Robert A. (1999), *The Struggle for Quebec* (Montreal: McGill-Queen's University Press).

GILES GHERSON
Comments on "The Politics of Paying for Cities in Canada"

ROBERT YOUNG'S ARTICLE ACKNOWLEDGES the mounting chorus of frustrated voices demanding that cities wrest more money and power from senior levels of government—mainly the provinces—consistent with their expanded stature. What are the pressures feeding the call for more money and autonomy for cities? These include globalization and the attendant rise of city states as significant and increasingly relevant economic, political and cultural jurisdictions around the world. Cities are more than ever concerned with trade and investment, immigration policy, criminal justice issues and economic competitiveness.

Another of the pressures is that of amalgamation, or the less formal "regionalization," of many Canadian cities with surrounding suburbs and exurbs into single super-cities with expanded scales of population, budgets and economic and political weight. Greater Edmonton, with a population of one million and a GDP of nearly $40 billion, is larger than six provinces. So are Toronto, Montreal, Vancouver, Ottawa-Hull and Calgary.

Young observes, primarily with reference to Toronto, that amalgamation may not only bring benefits and strength to cities. It can also boost inefficiency and add costs, as municipal employees' wages adjust upwards etc. So there are cross-cutting pressures. These include mounting municipal budget pressures from provincial "offloading," on the one hand, and reduced provincial transfers on the other. In recent years, provincial governments have restrained budget costs by offloading to municipalities some social service programs, including social housing, homeless shelters, after-school care, some parole supervision and so forth.

Just to take the last item, parole supervision, it is worth noting that because of the number of correctional institutions located in the Edmonton region, along with the extensive array of criminal justice-related services and the ready availability of well-paying blue-collar jobs due to the economic boom, Edmonton has the second largest number of parolees in the country, after Toronto. This has imposed considerable demands on the local police force that must be paid for by municipal taxpayers.

At the same time, provinces have curtailed fiscal transfers to cities—hence the "underfunding" trap that many cities now find themselves in. In the case of Edmonton, for example, the city in recent years has seen the removal of provincial transportation grants, policing grants and some unconditional grants. Provincial transfers to Edmonton in 1993 were $55 million—worth $75 million in today's dollars. But the city was to receive only $24 million in 2002 from the province which constitutes a pretty massive funding decline; this from a government famous for its attentiveness to public opinion. Young may be right to suggest that provincial governments seem to believe they have plenty of voters who aren't interested in paying for cities.

MUNICIPAL TAXING CONSTRAINTS

Another point about taxes and urban amalgamation: a key driver in the amalgamation campaigns in both Ottawa and Toronto was the need to shore up the relatively weak tax base of urban centres where many regional social and other services are located. By contrast, outlying communities often have a rich business-tax base yet relatively few expensive social services or transportation infrastructure demands to pay for. Amalgamation was definitely a way to spread regional fiscal capacity so that it better matches the provision of costly regional services, ending the implicit subsidy provided by urban centres to surrounding suburban communities.

Cities and Competitiveness

Even as they find themselves caught in a budget trap of reduced provincial funding and mounting spending demands, cities increasingly are under pressure to "be competitive" in attracting people and business investment. This is a powerful deterrent against higher taxes. Yet, at the same time, the chief source of city revenues—property taxes—happen to be far less responsive to economic growth than are federal and provincial income and sales taxes. Thus, despite competitiveness pressures, cities face constant pressure to boost rates to meet revenue shortfalls.

On the cost side, urban population growth from immigration and migration exert relentless pressures on social services, roads, housing, transit, police and emergency services, forcing painful budget choices on city politicians. Here in Edmonton, the city is talking right now about closing a library branch to help pay for the building of a suburban police station.

These cost and revenue pressures are placing Canada's larger cities under considerable financial strain, with potentially significant impacts on the quality of life experienced by the 80 per cent of Canadians who are city dwellers. But, despite the high stakes, Young argues that the most likely outcome, at least in the near term, will be no more than limited or incremental change in the way cities are financed. In other words, we are not on the cusp of some urban revolution or full-blown decolonialization of big cities as they throw off the shackles of their provincial masters and take their place as provincial equivalents. This despite the fact that Canada's top six cities—Toronto, Montreal, Vancouver, Ottawa-Hull, Calgary and Edmonton—have larger populations than a majority of the provinces. The reality is that all the brave talk of a "new deal for cities" (as Paul Martin phrases it) runs into some formidable institutional obstacles.

In our Constitution, cities are the creatures of provinces and prospects for a new municipal "third order" of government have to be rated at about nil. Provinces do not favour "big new policy changes," states Young, and, frankly, it's hard to see much evidence to the contrary. Despite fast-paced urban growth, institutionalized via amalgamation, provincial legislatures continue to be politically overweighted in favour of rural residents. Alberta is a good example. Cities are considerably underrepresented in the legislature and that helps keep cities down. Here's a lesson in political reality: the province of Alberta gave drought-stricken farmers a whopping $1 billion in relief in 2002–2003. Meanwhile, cities wonder when the province will throw $1 billion at them.

The federal government likes to flirt with cities—the ruling Liberals are heavily urban-based and their supporters identify strongly with urban issues; when the federal Liberal government is being ganged up against by a majority of provinces, party members fantasize about building a federal-urban coalition that would swamp the provinces. But the Liberals have been extremely cautious about treading on provincial turf and have instead emphasized working with the provinces on urban issues. The upshot has been plenty of sympathy but no federal assault on urban problems.

Moreover, it is fair to say that cities themselves have not mounted a coherent campaign to seize major tax power or jurisdictional autonomy from the provinces. Instead, as Young suggests, there has been a lot of loud grumbling and calls for larger transfers, some minor tax room (gasoline tax) and better consultation on urban matters by provincial governments. Considering Edmonton as an example, it is hard to argue with Young's basic thesis.

Edmonton is a rapidly expanding city with real growing pains, including a large and worsening infrastructure deficit (roads, bridges, transit); rising crime but a shortage of police officers; a fairly acute affordable housing shortage for working poor ; mounting pressure on social services; and a deteriorating downtown but few resources to spruce it up. Transfers from the province have fallen even as the city has filled in social services gaps. For the last several years, the province has provided Calgary and Edmonton with a cash grant equivalent to five cents a litre of the provincial gas tax, which has eased those cities' financial crunch. But while the province has now committed to providing this grant for the next three years, it cannot be counted on as a permanent revenue source. This was clear in 2002, when, facing financial pressures, the Klein government briefly reduced the grant and hinted it might cancel it altogether.

At the same time the city feels under enormous pressure to not raise property taxes, although it is evident that its tax rate is very much on the low side among large Canadian cities. Despite Young's scepticism about the benefits of amalgamation, there is some evidence that Greater Edmonton does suffer from its fragmentation. In other words, its present structure does impose costs which may become more acute as the city grows.

Greater Edmonton is made up of 22 municipalities. The region has two police forces (the Edmonton Police Service and the RCMP in surrounding communities), which inhibits crime fighting. It has several transit systems that don't mesh. Although there is regional water service, by and large the vast array of municipal services, from snow clearing and garbage removal to emergency services, is fragmented; Greater Edmonton does not speak to the provincial government (or outside investors) with one voice. There is a forum of mayors for regional discussion and cooperation called the Alberta Capital Region Association (ACRA), which meets on a regular basis. But local jealousies and an overriding suspicion on the part of the smaller municipalities that Edmonton simply wants to grab their tax base and take over their service delivery constrain its effectiveness. Ultimately, it is more of a talk shop than a substantive decisionmaking body.

Fairly intense investment competition among region's municipalities—each with its own economic development bureau—keeps taxes artificially low, perpetuating the perennial budget crisis. Edmonton itself, which faces the most severe budget squeeze, is constantly fretting about a further erosion of its business tax base to neighbouring municipalities if it raises property taxes. The government of Alberta has said it will not force amalgamation on Greater Edmonton and there seems to be little impetus among the municipalities surrounding Edmonton to further regionalize. Leduc County, Sturgeon County and Strathcona County are busy developing their own international trade and tourism identities and brands etc.

There is another reason to support Young's scepticism about major change: city councils by and large have not developed strong reputations for policy and administrative sophistication or depth. They are simply not seen as clear-sighted, competent problemsolvers. At least in Edmonton, city council is not good at fashioning strategies or plans and sticking to them, which I think creates a lack of confidence among the public. There is one major exception to this which is Edmonton's commendable record during the past seven to eight years for tight fiscal discipline tied to its no-debt strategy.

In the case of Edmonton, Young has read it right. The city would be pretty happy with more stable, predictable provincial funding; less provincial interference in issues like the municipally owned power company, EPCOR; less provincial offloading of social services; and greater collaboration with the province on decisionmaking. On the other hand, if Greater Edmonton ever did get its act together and created a strong regional metropolitan area, the combined clout of Calgary and Edmonton (with two-thirds of the province's population) could at the very least force concessions on a variety of fronts from a more accommodating provincial administration. But that still seems some way off.

Rapporteur: What Have We Learned?

MELVILLE L. McMILLAN

INTRODUCTION

MUNICIPAL GOVERNMENT HAS ONLY RECENTLY garnered much national attention, whether from the media, other governments, or academics. Notably, that attention has most recently focused on cities and, in particular, the financing of cities.[1] For those for whom municipal government is an important concern, it is encouraging to see the issues of municipalities and cities receiving more attention.

The contribution of the Institute for Public Economics to the discussion of these issues through the November 2002 conference at the University of Alberta is to be appreciated. As reflected by the lively exchanges, the articles presented afforded valuable background, interesting insights and sometimes controversial suggestions. The collection of essays, in combination with the discussants' comments, provides a provocative perspective on city financing and related problems from which those new to the topic and those experienced in these matters will both gain.

The range of matters addressed and the ideas advanced challenge a rapporteur. What has been learned will differ for each person because each brings a different background and different experiences. I will try to provide a summary of what most would consider the main points, but the result will reflect some of my own perspectives and opinions. Indeed, I will intentionally include some comments on what we have not heard but which I believe might have been included. My reflections are organized as follows. First, I will review the question of whether or not there a problem and, if so, what and how big. I will then review proposals for better rationalizing if not resolving the call for funding; that is, the paying-for-cities issue. The articles typically span and contribute to both these topics. A conclusion follows.

PAYING FOR CITIES: WHAT IS THE PROBLEM?

The widely cited factors felt to demonstrate the importance of cities and the difficulties that they are encountering are acknowledged by the contributors (e.g., see Kitchen). Examples include increasing urbanization, economic concentration in cities, their role in global competition, infrastructure demands (both new and for restoration), added responsibilities downloaded from other levels of government and reduced grants. While acknowledging these factors, many of the contributors look (sometimes more implicitly than explicitly) for evidence of a funding problem and the nature of that problem. The evidence appears to be mixed. Yes, there have been some changes but the problems may not be as serious or extensive as is sometimes suggested. But there is room for improvement.

It is often noted that 80 per cent of Canadians live in urban areas. Robert Young explores this concept further and finds that many of those Canadians live in small urban centres, leaving only 45 per cent living in cities with populations of more than 100,000. The result, he concludes, is that a large portion of the electorate is not interested in paying for cities, and especially the very large ones in which they do not live, through their provincial and federal taxes. This point also reflects what I consider to be an unduly narrow concern for cities and a neglect of other municipalities.

Infrastructure demands can put major financial pressures on cities. In growing cities, infrastructure is an up-front cost. Also, however, many cities are surprised by the magnitude of the outlays required to replace deteriorated infrastructure. The significance of these investments is emphasized by the fact that local governments, although they account for only a small fraction of total government spending (about 17 per cent in Canada), are typically responsible for half or more of the capital spending of all governments.

Alberta, and especially its cities, have experienced rapid growth during the past decade. Calgary's growth has been the most striking at about 41 per cent between 1991 and 2001, but even Edmonton, which was stalled early in the decade and for which much of the urban region's growth is in the surrounding communities, grew by 15 per cent. Yet even Calgary's growth fades in comparison to that of Edmonton's in the postwar years, which J.C. Herbert Emery reports as having doubled in population between 1946 and 1956. Cities were not better situated to cope with the demands of rapid population growth then than now and, as Albertans are well aware, they have managed to cope with periodic episodes of rapid growth in the past. As pointed out in the discussion, cities have often turned to development levies of various kinds to shift at least part of the new infrastructure demands onto the developers and, in turn, the eventual new property owners rather than local taxpayers.

Municipalities in Canada can only borrow for capital purposes and debt is typically an important source of their infrastructure finance. Interestingly, municipal debt and borrowing received limited attention. Indeed, the existing arrangements for debt finance—provincial supervision and provincial assistance provided for municipal borrowing—were not challenged.

Expenditures per capita of municipal governments show some interesting patterns and trends as Harry M. Kitchen and Ronald D. Kneebone and Kenneth J. McKenzie demonstrate. Between 1988–89 and 2001–2002 municipal per capita expenditures rose only 6.6 per cent in real (constant) dollars (or about 0.5 per cent per year) across Canada and even fell almost 15 per cent in Alberta. As a percentage of gross domestic provincial product (GDPP), municipal expenditures fell in all provinces but British Columbia and Ontario, and declined slightly for Canada as a whole from 4.6 per cent to 4.5 per cent. Municipal expenditures did rise somewhat relative to the provincial-local total, from 16.7 per cent to 17.3 per cent, as provincial spending declined over this period. If demands upon municipalities are pressing, they are not reflected in either absolutely or relatively growing expenditures.

The picture on the revenue side shows some interesting variations. Revenues have grown no faster than expenditures. Kitchen shows that municipal property taxes, the major source of municipal revenue, has declined across Canada as a percentage of GDPP since 1971–72—from 3.8 per cent to 2.3 per cent. However, looking at real per capita property taxes since 1988, those have risen from $662 to $789, or by almost 20 per cent and, as a percentage of disposable income (by my calculations), from 3.34 per cent to 3.69 per cent, which is a 10 per cent increase. Still, these are not large variations. In contrast, when the baby boom arrived in the schools, local property taxes surged from 3.1 per cent to 5.9 per cent of disposable income between 1947 and 1971 and, under that pressure, the provinces stepped in with substantially increased provincial grants for schooling. This reduced the burden to 4.6 per cent by 1980 and instituted a long-term shift in the local-provincial sharing of school funding (Kitchen and McMillan, 1985: 225). No such dramatic change in the property-tax burden that might spur provincial intervention is evidenced today.

Sources of funding are the major change in municipal revenues over the 1990s. Own revenues rose from 77 per cent to 83 per cent of total revenues while intergovernmental transfers (essentially all provincial) fell from 22.9 per cent to 17 per cent (1988 to 2001) and from over 25 per cent in the early 1990s. Provincial budget cuts aimed at eliminating provincial deficits came in part at the expense of municipal governments which had no one to pass the costs along to and share the burden. To a large extent, the dramatic reductions in transfers during the 1990s only served to emphasize the relatively persistent unreliability of grants as a revenue source. Intergovernmental transfer programs have periodically waxed and waned (not to mention the regular transformations of programs) depending, especially at the municipal level, upon the grantor's philosophy, whim and fiscal circumstances. Municipal governments are well aware of the volatility of transfers. When it comes to intergovernmental transfers, grantor governments are fickle friends.

To a very large extent, this reduction in grants must be what municipalities mean when they speak of provincial downloading. The references to the downloading, offloading, etc. of (mostly) provincial services to municipalities are widespread. Nevertheless, the documentation of significant instances has so far been weak, although some potentially interesting situations exist. The reduction in grants, however, is obvious, very real and, with a nationwide average reduction of 33 per cent within five years, substantial. Municipalities have responded with restrained expenditures and with some increases in property taxes and user charges.

Transportation is an area of municipal expenditure that several contributors point to as an anomaly. Transportation, notably road works, represents a major expenditure area at about 20 per cent of outlays. While provinces do share the cost of certain local transportation projects through grants, for the most part (the contributors have noted some exceptions), municipalities are expected to fund transportation costs from their own revenues (predominately the property tax) while receiving no revenue from vehicle-related taxes. Vehicle-related taxes such as fuel taxes and registration fees are the domain of and flow to the provincial and the federal governments. Emery observes that road expenditures by local governments from 1951 to 1976 grew faster and far exceeded those of the provincial governments. Although a relatively casual inspection, data that I have reviewed suggest that the provincial share of transportation expenditures has continued to decline, and decline substantially, relative to that of municipal governments over the 1968 to 2000 period. That the level of government responsible for the majority of road expenditures should have little or no access to vehicle-related taxes is peculiar in that it is at odds with the principle of benefit taxation that is paramount at the local level.

Certainly, since 1988 municipal governments have restrained spending and been forced to rely increasingly upon their own sources of revenue. The slow grow of expenditures and even local taxes may be seen as evidence that the fiscal situation of municipalities is not acute. Let it be noted, however, that the past decade or more did not provide a hospitable environment for expanding local budgets. First, real disposable incomes rose only slowly, certainly no faster than municipal expenditures, so taxpayers have been particularly mindful of governments encroaching upon disposable income even to the modest extent of municipal government.

Second, both the federal and provincial governments were into serious budget reductions and their actions and words, particularly in Alberta where the provincial government was most vociferous, threw an ominous shadow over the local government sector and any municipal government considering anything other than expenditure restrictions and tax cuts. Hence, one must be careful about interpreting these developments as evidence that there is no problem with municipal finance, or even that the problems that exist are small. Almost a decade of restraint may have been accomplished by deferring sensible infrastructure replacement and repair. Failing to provide services that many consider not only desirable but are badly needed may cost us more later. In addition, the issue may not be that the current situation is getting significantly worse but rather that people see, or even just feel, that there are alternatives for paying for cities that would yield improvements.

PAYING FOR CITIES: WHAT ARE THE OPTIONS?

The evidence cited in the previous section suggests that the problem of paying for cities may not be as serious as it is sometimes presented. This is not to suggest that meeting the demands for municipal services is not a concern or that improvements might not be made. In this section, I review important options and consider the numerous suggestions made by the contributors. Initially, however, I will proceed from the comparison of municipal services and financing provided especially by Kitchen and by Kneebone and McKenzie to highlight certain critical elements of a framework upon which to reflect on the alternatives. That section is followed by an overview of the major financing alternatives.

A Framework for Reflection

In undertaking this review of various proposals for enhancing municipal finance, it is useful to state up front the core criteria upon which I intend to base my comments. My first criterion is that finance follows function. This criterion requires an appreciation of the services that municipal governments are to supply. My second criterion is that there must be a clear benefit-cost linkage in municipal finance; that is, the tie between benefits received and costs borne, while important for all levels of government, is especially so for municipal government. Dahlby's comments pursue the criteria issue further.

Consider initially the functional responsibilities of municipal government in Canada. It is interesting and worthwhile to reflect briefly upon the geographic pattern of expenditures across the provinces. Per capita expenditure is relatively modest in the Atlantic provinces (especially when one allows for the unusual contribution to education by Nova Scotia's municipalities) in comparison with other provinces. Without going into any detail, it is hardly surprising that local governments in larger provinces are delegated greater responsibilities. Note too that Ontario—a "distinct society," as Kneebone and McKenzie write, quoting earlier work by Kitchen—is somewhat different from the other provinces.

Ontario has a tradition of putting relatively large financial responsibilities upon its local governments. The "reforms" under the Harris government did not change that, although they did transform the responsibilities to a considerable degree. Unlike in the other provinces, and contrary to the recommendations of most authorities in the field, Ontario municipalities have borne and now bear an even larger responsibility for social services. Thus, to a considerable degree, there are the Atlantic provinces, Ontario, and the rest. Alberta is not that much different from the rest, other than perhaps being on the high end of the per capita spending scale. It is valuable to keep interprovincial differences in mind when looking at municipal, as well as other, data.

After reviewing municipal budgets in the Canadian provinces, Kneebone and McKenzie conclude that recent experience gives us little guidance for determining optimal expenditure and revenue responsibilities. While perhaps they choose some poetic licence for emphasis, I would caution against accepting their conclusion(s) without further reflection. A more comprehensive review over a longer time frame might suggest that, despite the diversity and some clear areas of concern, municipal finance and services in Canada are more rationally structured than it may seem at first glance (e.g., see McMillan, forthcoming a and b).

Kitchen provides a convenient extension for illustration. If the five states upon which he reports are representative, municipal governments in the United States make much higher outlays for municipal services than do Canadian municipalities and, in addition, their expenditures and revenue sources can also be quite different among states and in comparison to those of Canadian municipalities.[2] Is the U.S. model necessarily better or worse?

Even with the distinctions noted, there is not a large variation in the roles of municipal governments across Canada. International comparison demonstrates greater, and often wide, diversity. The range is particularly striking if the roles of local government generally are considered. While we focus on municipalities separate from schools (and other possible local authorities), municipalities in many countries encompass schooling and also have major responsibilities for health care and other social services. When the range of responsibilities are so wide and the responsibilities differ so much, no one financing model is appropriate for all local governments. For local government to function effectively and efficiently in these various circumstances, the financial structure must be designed to suit the responsibilities assigned: that is, finance follows function.

While there is reference to the potential for the expansion of municipal government responsibilities (e.g., into health care, along the lines of the

Swedish model) and of the problems of school finance via a property tax (e.g., O'Brien, Young), the consensus is that municipal representatives have little interest in broadening municipal responsibilities as opposed to securing better financing for existing tasks. This perspective simplified the task of the November 2002 "Paying for Cities" conference and focused the work and recommendations of the contributors.

Even our large urban municipalities are, with rare exceptions, relatively small geographically and people are mobile. Hence, the benefits from municipal services must be seen to correspond closely to municipal taxes and charges or people will move to jurisdictions that are fiscally more attractive. In addition, it is widely recognized that local funding for local services is the basis of a clear benefit-cost linkage in local (as well as other) jurisdictions, which also promotes the accountability of the local elected decisionmakers to their constituents. Advocating local funding for local service does not deny that a valid case can be made for equalizing transfers on both equity and efficiency grounds. Calling for a clear link between benefits and costs also permits recognition of interjurisdictional spillovers, the role of transfers to generate the proper prices and incentives in the presence of spillovers, and defines the role of overlying (e.g., provincial) government.

Financing Options

I examine the financing options under three categories: those that simply tweak the exiting system; following the lead of Kneebone and McKenzie, those that are relatively modest proposals; and finally, some immodest proposals.

Tweaking the Existing System

I group here the various suggestions from the contributors that I see as adjustments to the existing municipal finance system in Canada as part of efforts to make it fairer, more efficient and/or more effective at generating revenue. Improvements to the property taxes, business taxes and user charges are the main focus for Kitchen; Kneebone and McKenzie also critically analyze these. In regards to property taxes, the discussion largely centres on the potential disincentives associated with the taxation of land and improvements versus land alone and the typically differential treatment of residential versus business property (in favour of residential property). Furthermore, the extensive taxation of business beyond the property tax through specific business taxes (for which Canadian levels are notable internationally) draws considerable discussion. The potential for further utilization and reliance upon user fees is advocated.

These issues and the related concerns, criticisms and recommendations are relatively standard fare in the economists' assessment of local revenues.

Although conventional, they are no less relevant. In instances, improvements have been made. While there is still ample room for further developments, economists are pleased to see the growing importance of user fees in municipal budgets. Economists, however, can expect a continuing and uphill struggle in their efforts to enhance the efficiency of the existing municipal tax-revenue system.

As both Edward C. LeSage and Young point out in their comments, politics is a nonmarket activity and the political processes and "political efficiency," not economic efficiency, are the main players in arriving at the final decisions on these choices. Both politicians and citizens are often sceptical of recommendations to expand user fees and/or shift a larger share of the tax burden to residential property in order to improve efficiency (even when there is no tax exporting involved and the local residents ultimately pay the total costs).

During the sessions, observations were made about why the provinces were collecting property taxes. Where the provinces centralized school finances by effectively stripping school boards of their taxing powers, it was convenient to take over the school property taxes to fund the expanded provincial school grants.[3] However, if school finances are to be provincialized, there is little logic in relying upon (at least general) property taxes to fund education when superior taxes are available at the provincial level. Nevertheless, even if the provinces were to abandon general property taxes, it is unlikely to represent a tax-room godsend for municipalities. Local taxpayers, it seems, distinguish between school and municipal taxes and judge the levels of each on their respective merits.

The contributors and commentators say relatively little about the potential for rationalizing grants to municipalities. I will make a small attempt to rectify that omission. Too often, provincial and federal governments have seen transfers (often evidenced in a multiplicity of transfers) to municipalities as a means of providing general support when it is convenient to do so. Economically, grants have well-identified purposes; that is, to close a fiscal gap, to correct for spillovers and to equalize fiscal capacities. Fiscal gaps are difficult to measure and there is little evidence here of any fiscal gap at the municipal level. Even if there was, there are very likely superior ways for closing any gap (a point I hope will become evident in subsequent discussion). Hence, we pass over the fiscal gap reason here. The spillovers of benefits from locally generated services will result in underprovision—a problem that appropriately designed grants can correct. Transportation often provides good examples of spillovers and, frequently, grants are provided in efforts to offset those externalities.

I suspect that efforts to better recognize and measure spillovers could result in superior grants in transportation and in other areas. Policing, especially the crime-control side (as opposed to local traffic control, bylaw enforcement, etc.) often has a significant externality component to it but, in some provinces, grants are not provided to cities to reflect the broader benefits resulting from local policing expenditures. Shelters for the homeless (for whom cities feel obliged to provide some minimal service if for no other reason than because the homeless reside on city streets), represents another area for which transfers may be inadequate. Housing for the elderly might be a related area. If the provinces and the federal governments, in conjunction with the municipalities, carefully reviewed their municipal transfers, paying close attention to spillovers, superior transfer systems might result.

Equalization grants for reducing fiscal disparities (particularly for the most disadvantaged municipalities) are another area of municipal transfers that could be reviewed. Alberta terminated its equalizing transfers during its deficit-elimination exercise. O'Brien suggests that Alberta should consider restoring those equalizing transfers. When cities and other municipalities call for more attention to their fiscal needs, a joint review of the rationale for and levels of provincial and federal transfers could prove valuable. Logical and carefully designed transfer programs structured on a sound base and using better measures would enable local government to operate more effectively and make it more difficult for the granting government to vary its funding at its convenience. Hence, a more stable, more reliable and, for some programs, a more efficient source of revenue could result.[4] While grant reform may rationalize transfers, it is unlikely to result in major increases in funding to municipal governments.

The Modest Proposals

In this section, I focus on Kitchen's proposal for tax-exempt bonds and the proposals (most extensively discussed by Kneebone and McKenzie) for municipal vehicle fuel taxes (and other vehicle taxes). Other possibilities exist and are posed in the articles but I concentrate on these two because the one seems unattractive while the other has gathered some support but calls for further consideration.

Kitchen suggests that municipal bonds be exempted from income taxes. Such a move would in effect be a transfer from provincial and federal governments to borrowing municipal governments; that is, because Canadian local governments can only issue bonds (borrow) for capital purposes, such an exemption would act as a subsidy to debt-financed capital expenditures. As such, it introduces a number of distortions. It distorts incentives to investors, it encourages municipalities to rely more upon debt for capital finance and it encourages municipalities to substitute capital investment for operating costs. Economists in the United States, where the interest from municipal bonds is tax exempt, frequently criticize this concession. The idea has also been frowned upon in Canada by the TD Financial Group (2002).

If one were to consider income-tax concessions, an alternative might be more attractive. Somewhat reluctantly, I have suggested that property taxes that currently are not tax deductible—essentially, residential property taxes on owner-occupied housing—could become eligible for a refundable personal income-tax credit (say at the minimum positive personal income-tax rates) by both federal and provincial governments. Doing so would provide (owner occupant) residential property taxpayers with a refund that might amount to about 20 per cent to 25 per cent of their residential property taxes. Thus, all residential property taxes paid by owner occupants would be shared with the federal and provincial governments (regardless of the taxpayers' income) making the property taxes of this group less onerous and opening the potential for expanded property tax use to a significant share of municipal voters.

One could speculate, however, about how much of this concession would find its way into municipal coffers and, ultimately, expenditures in contrast to a grant of equal cost to the provincial and federal governments. Unlike a concession for municipal bond interest, this concession would not distort the use of the funds generated. In fact, the relative neutrality of this concession makes it relatively attractive. Furthermore, to a large extent, this provision would serve to remove the current disparity (and economic distortion) in the treatment of business (including rental residential) property taxes (which are tax deductible) and that of owner-occupied residential property taxes (which are nondeductible), an issue raised in the conference discussion. It would, on the other hand, subsidize property taxes relative to other forms of municipal own revenues and could distort that choice.

The importance of transportation outlays to municipalities and the lack of municipal vehicle-related revenues is noted by various contributors to this volume, as well as by others during the discussion. This anomaly detracts from the benefit relationship considered so important for municipal finance. There is a clear logic for municipal access to vehicle fuel-tax revenues. The logic of having individual municipalities determine and levy their own vehicle fuel taxes is, however, weaker. Vehicles are obviously highly mobile and drivers can easily travel to avoid local fuel taxes.

The possibilities for avoidance are greatest in multijurisdictional communities. Undoubtedly, some municipalities will find gas stations more attractive than local fuel taxes. Even for large municipalities (or where regional associations of municipalities can agree to cooperate) where travel costs are greater, border problems persist. An obvious border problem situation would arise should cities, but not the surrounding (e.g., rural) municipalities, be permitted to levy fuel taxes. The social costs of the individually attractive behaviour to avoid taxes and the distortion of business location would not be trivial. Border problems already exist at provincial boundaries; for example, Lloydminster, where the Saskatchewan fuel tax is graduated with distance from the Alberta border. Where local fuel taxes are in place in Canada (e.g., the Greater Vancouver Regional District), they are provincially determined. Vehicle fuel taxes are an excellent candidate for revenue-sharing.

The provinces (also the federal government) already collect substantial fuel-tax revenues. A portion of these (and also registration) revenues could easily be shared with all municipalities. Note the emphasis on *all* municipalities. Transportation outlays are often more significant for rural than urban municipalities. There is little logic, as in Alberta's case (although it is a good start), to share provincial vehicle revenues only with cities (or, even more so, only certain cities such as Edmonton and Calgary).

If municipalities were allowed to levy municipal vehicle taxes, vehicle registration charges would be a reasonable option. Owners of vehicles live in a particular municipality and, to a large extent, use their vehicles there. Residence is relatively immobile so a locally determined vehicle registration is less easily escaped (especially if significant fines accompany improper registration). Commercial vehicles used primarily outside the "home" community could be levied a representative supplementary provincial registration fee to be shared among municipalities. To minimize administration and compliance costs, such a tax should be "piggy-backed" on the provincial registration system.

Tolls on road use are another possibility. Tolls are best suited, especially for cities, for controlling congestion. Technology is making the use of tolls more feasible; for example, London, England, has introduced tolls on central city traffic. The extensive use of tolls in Canada in the near future, however, seems unlikely.

For vehicle-related taxes, fuel taxes (and possibly registration charges) are good candidates for provincial and, indeed, even federal government revenue-sharing with all municipalities. As a tax that municipalities might individually determine, local registration fees are more attractive than local fuel taxes. These conclusions are, I believe, reasonably consistent with Kneebone and McKenzie, although they may be of the opinion that there is more potential for locally levied fuel taxes than I believe to be the case or at least advisable.

The Immodest Proposals
In this category, I highlight and address two essentially revenue-sharing proposals from Kneebone and McKenzie, and also the potential for two new municipal tax sources—a general sales tax and a local income tax, noted particularly by Kitchen.

Kneebone and McKenzie suggest eliminating or, at least, very much scaling back existing provincial grants to the cities/municipalities and replacing those funds with a form of revenue-sharing transfer funded by increased sales taxes. In order to be revenue neutral to the province, the increased sales-tax revenue would be offset by reducing the personal income tax. In Alberta's case, a two per cent sales tax (piggy-backed on the GST, I assume) would substitute for a two percentage point reduction in the provincial PIT rate. The merits of this change are argued to be the efficiency gains from a shift from personal income taxes to consumption taxes.

Kneebone and McKenzie also suggest replacing municipal business taxes with shared revenue from a provincial business value-added tax (BVT). The merit of this idea is that a BVT is more neutral and more efficient than the multiplicity of municipal business taxes. Municipal business taxes are relatively high in Canada and they have been widely criticized.

These two proposals are revenue-sharing programs and, as such, have the problems common to revenue-sharing. In addition, because the shared funds merely substitute for other (provincial or own) funds, they really offer nothing for the municipalities. The programs look more like provincial tax-reform programs than proposals to assist municipalities. Unlike most revenue-sharing programs, these do not offer additional or new money for municipalities. In the case of the BVT substituting for municipal business taxes, local control over finances would actually diminish.

Before embarking on such a scheme, it would be valuable to assess more fully the actual distortion and welfare loss due to local business taxation. Might municipal decisionmakers actually be relatively efficient taxers and tax inelastic versus elastic business sources; that is, craft their taxes in a form of niche taxation? If business capital is as mobile as suggested, decisionmakers may be well aware of the consequences of poor business tax decisions and avoid them. In the case of totally replacing existing grants with revenue-sharing, the purposes for intergovernmental grants (other than gap closing) that were noted above are ignored. While the existing provincial (and federal) municipal grants can easily be faulted, overlooking the efficiency rationale for grants may result in no efficiency gain.

Revenue-sharing programs necessarily cause debate on how the revenue is to be shared. Focusing upon cities seems too narrow. If general taxes are to generate the shared revenue, all municipalities will need to be included in the distribution. Not all municipalities rely on business taxes. Distribution to origin of both BVT or sales taxes will disadvantage jurisdictions with few market outlets (i.e., rural municipalities). As Dahlby notes, revenue-sharing also raises concern about accountability. Municipal authorities will want and will pressure for revenue-sharing to be enhanced. General-purpose shared revenue reduces the benefit-cost link of the municipal citizen-taxpayer.

Finally, while consumption and value-added are moderately stable revenue sources, there are economic fluctuations and, like other grants, they are not immune to political intervention.[5] Nevertheless, revenue-sharing has some appeal and has some history even in Canada, although the level of support provided has typically been small. If revenue-sharing with municipalities is to be introduced, it is probably best that it be planned and designed explicitly as a revenue-sharing program.

Municipalities might be better served by an expanded tax base.[6] One possibility is a municipal general sales tax. By this we refer to municipalities being able to set a sales tax rate to be applied within their jurisdiction by piggy-backing it onto a provincial sales tax or the federal GST. Local general sales taxes are not uncommon in the United States but not often found elsewhere beyond southern Europe. Local sales taxes can raise considerable revenue and, in part for this reason, have attracted some attention and support in Canada.[7] They account for about ten per cent of local tax revenue in the United States. There are, however, numerous criticisms of local sales taxes. They affect consumers choice of where to buy and so business location decisions. Hence, the problems noted previously concerning local vehicle-fuel taxes reappear.

Because sales are normally concentrated in urban areas, local sales taxes work to the disadvantage of rural areas and may result in some exporting of urban costs to rural residents. Sales taxes are often not comprehensive and fail to tax services as effectively as goods. For these reasons, sales taxes may (again) be better suited as a source of funding for revenue-sharing programs. Because these costs of sales taxes are in many cases somewhat obscure, sales taxes may seem more attractive than warranted. The trade-offs are not entirely clear and will differ with the particular circumstances.

Municipal personal income taxes are another option. Although frequently overlooked, local income taxes are not that unusual. They are the mainstay of municipal government in the Scandinavian countries but municipal government there has much greater responsibilities and especially so in the social services area. In the United States, which more closely parallels the Canadian situation, about 3,700 local governments apply local income taxes (versus 6,500 using sales taxes) and local income taxes generate 5.9 per cent of local tax revenue (versus 10 per cent for local sales taxes). Local income taxes are used by at least some municipalities in each of the five states that Kitchen offers for comparison in his Table 4. Municipal income taxes are a particularly popular and important revenue source for cities in the United States. Canadian municipalities only lost their income-tax powers with the 1941 federal-provincial tax rental agreement.

A municipal income tax would typically be levied at a low flat rate on the personal income of residents. A one per cent rate is not atypical. Corporate income is not taxed due to tax exporting problems although, to capture personal income comprehensively, the income of professional corporations and small corporations may need to be included. The treatment of commuters varies and is debatable. Income taxes offer some advantages for municipalities. To keep administrative and compliance costs low, they can easily be piggy-backed on provincial income taxes.

Because the tax and the benefits it helps finance is based upon residence, a municipal personal income tax, like the property tax (and unlike local sales taxes), is relatively nondistorting as a local revenue source. It provides a potentially significant tax source that, unlike the property tax (or sales taxes), relates closely to ability to pay which may facilitate a better matching of benefits and costs at the municipal level. Unlike sales taxes, neither rural nor urban municipalities are disadvantaged by access to municipal income taxes. It is also, like the property and sales taxes, visible. This is a feature that economists, concerned about accountability, might appreciate more than local politicians.

On the negative side, a municipal income tax (like the local fuel or sales taxes) would add a third tax authority to a shared base which might, as Dahlby notes, result in undesirable fiscal externalities. Also, income taxes are, at a "national" level, more distorting to incentives than sales or property taxes. Which tax would correspond most closely to the benefits of municipal services has not been determined.

Although he ultimately downplays the potential of municipal income taxes (it appears, because of expected unpopularity with provincial and federal governments), Kitchen does a service through his discussion of them. Too often in the discussion of municipal finances, they are ignored or avoided (e.g., Vander Ploeg, January and September, 2002) or cavalierly dismissed (e.g., TD Bank, 2002). If decisionmakers are to make the best decisions, they need the most complete and the best information available.

CONCLUSION

Despite the increased attention directed towards cities and their finances, there is no compelling evidence that cities are in dire financial straits or that paying for cities is an acute problem. However, cities and municipal governments, generally, have not had an easy time in recent years. Provincial transfers to cities have been sharply reduced. In addition, federal and provincial service cutbacks have placed new demands on cities that many feel require addressing. Furthermore, the political and economic environments have been inhospitable for municipal governments now required to rely increasingly upon their own revenues (i.e., higher taxes to maintain services).

In addition, while aided by an improved economy, federal and provincial governments have been able to eliminate deficits and, in some cases, even reduce taxes while cities have not shared in those gains. Cities even find that growth creates additional demands for their services. Overall, the attention and concern expressed may not result from municipalities and notably cities experiencing, for example, dramatic increases in tax burdens but, rather, that there is a feeling that they are not getting their share, that they want more stability in funding, that they could have greater control over their affairs and that there are better ways to meet the fiscal demands placed upon them.

In considering the options for paying for cities, the "Paying for Cities" conference posed no real challenge to the property tax and user charges as an appropriate base for financing the functions of Canadian municipalities. This is, in part, because they afford a strong benefit-cost linkage between those paying for services and those benefiting from them. However, there is no shortage of suggestions for how these traditional sources might be modified or "tweaked" to make them perform better (as well as suggestions for improving intergovernmental transfers). Recognizing the magnitude of capital spending by municipal government and the importance of borrowing to finance infrastructure led to a suggestion for provincial and federal governments to provide income-tax concessions to municipal bond interest. This idea raised various concerns and prompted me to suggest that, if there were to be tax concessions, consideration be given to refundable income-tax credits for property taxes that are currently not deductible for income-tax purposes.

The articles and the discussion at the conference indicate widespread agreement that cities (and municipalities generally) should receive a share of vehicle-related taxes. Although road transportation expenditures are a major cost for municipalities, municipalities receive almost no revenue (beyond parking fees) related to the vehicles and the users of roadways. That municipalities share in vehicle-fuel taxes and/or registration fees is logical. Provincial and/or federal revenue-sharing appears most practical for fuel taxes but, alternatively, municipalities could be allowed to determine their own registration fees (to be collected along with the provincial fees).

Two other proposals for revenue-sharing were advanced. One would replace existing transfers to municipalities with new provincial sales tax-financed shared revenue (offset at the provincial level by lower income taxes). The other would replace municipal business-tax revenue with shared revenue from a new business value-added tax. While these two proposals may have some merit as avenues of provincial tax reform, neither appeared to offer anything for municipalities. In addition, arriving at suitable sharing arrangements could be challenging.

Government-citizen accountability suggests that if cities/municipalities are fiscally stressed, new tax sources could be the best option. To raise significant amounts of funds to augment or partially substitute for existing own-source revenues leads to the choice between a local general sales tax or a local personal income tax. There is considerable experience elsewhere with both but neither is ideal. Because residents are less mobile than shoppers, the edge might go to an income tax, leaving the sales tax, like (and for the same reasons) the fuel tax, for revenue-sharing. If revenue-sharing is the route to follow, perhaps revenue-sharing through the income tax system (i.e., refundable tax credits for nondeductible property taxes) that leaves the decisions at the local level deserves serious consideration. It avoids the sharing formula problem and is probably more stable in that it is likely more difficult than other transfers for the income-taxing governments to reduce.

Many suggestions were made at the conference. Will any be acted upon? The political scientists in the group are pessimistic, arguing that the federal and provincial governments have shown little real interest and prefer, and have intentionally designed, municipal governments to be relatively weak. However, they do acknowledge that some positive prospects do exist. Will those prospects emerge to enhance municipal government in the future? Central to the issue of paying for cities is whether other levels of government are of the view that the existing sources of own-revenues and existing transfers are inadequate or inappropriate for meeting the current responsibilities of cities.

Notes

1. Note particularly Prime Minister's Caucus Task Force on Urban Issues (2002), TD Bank Financial Group (2002) and Vander Ploeg (January and September, 2002).
2. See Kitchen's Table 4 in this volume. Note the need to distinguish between municipal and school data.
3. I tend to agree with O'Brien, as I understood his comments, that the provinces overstepped themselves in their full provincialization of school finances. I feel that, in making that move, the provinces did themselves and schooling a disservice. Their efforts would have been better spent to improve the equalization system, centralize school property taxes on industrial and commercial property, and leave school boards with tax authority on residential and farm (ideally, farm residential) property.
4. Reforms to provide more stability to transfers to municipalities is likely to also prove an uphill climb.
5. Calgary and Edmonton almost lost their share of the fuel tax shortly after the program was introduced.
6. See McMillan (forthcoming, a and b) for more detail.
7. Note particularly, TD Bank Financial Group (2002).

References

Kitchen, Harry M. and Melville L. McMillan (1985), "Local Government and Canadian Federalism," in vol. 63 of Studies for the Royal Commission on the Economic Union and Development Prospects for Canada, Richard Simeon, ed., *Intergovernmental Relations* (Toronto: University of Toronto Press), 215–61.

McMillan, Melville L. (forthcoming a), "Designing Local Governments for Performance," chap. 11 in vol. 5 of the Handbook on Public Sector Performance Reviews, Robin Boadway and Anwar Shah, eds., *Fiscal Federalism: Principles and Practices* (Oxford: Oxford University Press for the World Bank).

——— (forthcoming b), "A Local Perspective on Fiscal Federalism," chap. 7 in vol. 6 of the Handbook on Public Sector Performance Reviews, Anwar Shah, ed., *Macrofederalism and Local Finances* (Oxford: Oxford University Press for the World Bank).

Prime Minister's Caucus Task Force on Urban Issues (2002), Canada's Urban Strategy: A Blueprint for Action, Chair: Judy Sgro, November.

TD Bank Financial Group (2002), The Choice between Investing in Canada's Cities or Disinvesting in Canada's Future, TD Economics Special Report, www.td.com/economics, http://www.td.com/economics, April.

Vander Ploeg, C. (2002), "Big City Revenue Sources: A Canada-U.S. Comparison of Municipal Tax Tools and Revenue Levers," (Calgary: Canada West Foundation).

——— (2002), "Framing a Fiscal Fix-Up: Options for Strengthening the Finances of Western Canada's Big Cities"(Calgary: Canada West Foundation, January).

Contributors

PAUL BOOTHE is Professor of Economics and Director of the Institute for Public Economics at the University of Alberta. His current research interests include fiscal relations between governments and health-care financing. Boothe received his undergraduate training in Economics at the University of Western Ontario and his doctoral degree from the University of British Columbia. He served as Deputy Minister of Finance and Secretary to Treasury Board for the province of Saskatchewan from 1999 to 2001, and has held visiting positions at Queen's University, the University of Tasmania and Alberta Treasury. Boothe has authored or edited numerous books and monographs, including *Deficit Reduction in the Far West* (University of Alberta Press, 2001), *Finding a Balance: Renewing Canadian Fiscal Federalism* (C.D. Howe Institute, 1998) and *Reforming Fiscal Federalism for Global Competition* (University of Alberta Press, 1996). Boothe is the C.D. Howe Institute's EnCana Scholar in Public Policy.

BEV DAHLBY is Professor of Economics at the University of Alberta. He attended the University of Saskatchewan, Queen's University and the London School of Economics. Dahlby has published extensively on tax policy and fiscal federalism. He has served as a policy advisor to the federal and provincial governments, as technical advisor on an International Monetary Fund mission to Malawi, and has worked on tax-reform projects at the Thailand Development Research Institute in Bangkok. Dahlby was a member of the Technical Committee on Business Taxation (the Mintz Committee) and has also served as an Associate Editor of *Canadian Public Policy* and as a member of the editorial board of the *Canadian Tax Journal*. From 1998 to 1999, he held a McCalla Research Professorship at the University of Alberta and in August 2002 was the Abe Greenbaum Visiting Fellow at the Australian Taxation Studies Program, University of New South Wales.

J.C. HERBERT EMERY received his BA (Honours) in Economics from Queen's University in 1988 and his PhD in Economics from the University of British Columbia in 1993. He has taught at the University of Calgary since 1993. Emery is the co-author (with George Emery) of *A Young Man's Benefit: The*

Independent Order of Odd Fellows and Sickness Insurance in the United States and Canada, 1860–1929 (McGill-Queen's University Press, 1999). He was the recipient (with Kenneth J. McKenzie) of the Harry Johnson Prize for the best article in the *Canadian Journal of Economics* (1996).

GILES GHERSON is Editor-in-Chief of the *Edmonton Journal*. He is the former Editor-in-Chief of Southam News and Political Editor of the *National Post*; in 1996 he was the National Economics Columnist for Southam News; in 1993, the National Political Correspondent for *The Globe and Mail*; and from 1989 to 1993 the Ottawa bureau chief and national columnist for *The Financial Times*. Gherson has contributed chapters to *The Free Trade Deal* (1988) and *Canada Among Nations* (1992). He has won several national journalism awards, including the Public Policy Forum's 1993 Hyman Solomon Award for Excellence in Public Policy Journalism, and has appeared as a commentator on numerous radio and television programs.

HARRY M. KITCHEN is Professor of Economics at Trent University. His research interests include Canadian taxation and public policy issues, local government revenues and expenditures. Kitchen is the author of *Municipal Revenue and Expenditure Issues in Canada* (2002), *Canadian Tax Policy*, 3rd ed., with Robin Boadway (1999), and numerous articles, monographs and reports on local government finance, expenditures and organizational issues. He is a member of the Urban Finance Advisory Committee of the Canada West Foundation and the editorial board of the *Canadian Tax Journal*.

RONALD D. KNEEBONE is Professor of Economics at the University of Calgary. His research interests include the macroeconomic aspects of public finances, political economy and fiscal federalism. Kneebone is the co-author (with N.G. Mankiw, Kenneth J. McKenzie and N. Rowe) of *Principles of Microeconomics and Principles of Macroeconomics*. In 1999 he shared (with Kenneth J. McKenzie) the Douglas Purvis Memorial Prize for a published work of excellence relating to Canadian public policy. In current research, he is investigating the issue of deficit offloading between levels of government in a federation and the nature of budgeting choices under fiscal stress. Kneebone is an Associate Editor of *Canadian Public Policy*.

EDWARD C. LESAGE is Professor of Extension at the University of Alberta and has served as Director of Government Studies in the Faculty of Extension since 1975. His areas of academic specialization are governance, local government and public administration. LeSage received his PhD in Political Science from Carleton University. LeSage has served as a consultant and advisor to governments, local government management professional associations and programs and institutes of local government. He has served on the national executive of the Institute of Public Administration, the executive group of the Canadian Association for Programs in Public Administration and the advisory board of the University of Victoria's Local Government Institute.

KENNETH J. MCKENZIE is Professor of Economics at the University of Calgary. He received his BComm from the University of Saskatchewan, his MA from the University of Calgary and his PhD from Queen's University. His research interests include public economics, with an emphasis on taxation and political economy. In 2000 McKenzie was the recipient of the Faculty of Social Sciences Distinguished Research Award at the University of Calgary. He was awarded (with J.C. Herbert Emery) the Harry Johnson Prize for the best article in the *Canadian Journal of Economics* (1996), and (with Ronald D. Kneebone) the Douglas Purvis Memorial Prize (1999). McKenzie holds research fellowships at the C.D. Howe Institute and the Fraser Institute and is the Editor of *Canadian Public Policy*.

MELVILLE L. MCMILLAN is a Professor in the Department of Economics and a Fellow of the Institute of Public Economics at the University of Alberta. He served as Chair of the Department from 1987 to 1997. His BA and MSc are from the University of Alberta and his PhD is from Cornell University. Before joining the University of Alberta in 1975, McMillan was on the faculty of the University of Wisconsin (Madison). His research and teaching interests are in public economics: in particular, urban and local economics, fiscal federalism and the demand for and supply of public goods and services. These interests were the focus of his research while on leaves at the Australian National University, Canberra, and the University of York, England. He has published extensively in these areas and also advised governments and organizations nationally and internationally, including the World Bank. McMillan is on the editorial board of the *Canadian Tax Journal*.

ALLISON D. O'BRIEN is a fellow of the Institute for Public Economics and a senior fellow of the C.D. Howe Institute. He retired as Deputy Provincial Treasurer of the province of Alberta in May 1999 after a 35-year career in Alberta Treasury. He received the Lieutenant Governor's Award for Exceptional Achievement and Distinctive Leadership in Public Administration in Alberta in 1998. O'Brien received his BA (Honours) and MA in Economics from the University of Alberta. He is a director of the Alberta Treasury Branches and IFPT Management Inc., and a public member of the Council of the Institute of Chartered Accountants of Alberta.

ROBERT YOUNG is Professor in the Department of Political Science at the University of Western Ontario. He holds a Canada Research Chair in Multilevel

Governance, and currently is president of the Canadian Political Science Association. He has studied many areas of politics and public policy, including Maritimes politics, trade and industrial policy, and federalism and public administration. His current interests include municipal-federal-provincial relations. For the past few years, Young has concentrated on Quebec politics and the issues raised by secession. He is the author of *The Breakup of Czechoslovakia* (1994), *The Secession of Quebec and the Future of Canada* (1995; 2nd ed. 1998) and *The Struggle for Quebec* (1999), and the editor of *Stretching the Federation: The Art of the State in Canada* (1999).